How to Write Better Business Letters

Fifth Edition

Andrea B. Geffner, M.A.

Former Dean

Taylor Business Institute, New York

President

ESCO, Inc., New York

Excerpted in part from *Business English, Fourth Edition: A Complete Guide to Developing an Effective Business Writing Style* by Andrea B. Geffner, and *Business Letters the Easy Way* by Andrea Geffner

Published by Kaplan, Inc., d/b/a Barron's Educational Series
750 Third Avenue
New York, NY 10017
www.barronseduc.com

Library of Congress Catalog Card No. 2012037072

ISBN: 978-1-4380-0137-1

Library of Congress Cataloging-in-Publication Data
Geffner, Andrea B.
    How to write better business letters / Andrea B. Geffner.—5th ed.
        p. cm.
    Includes index.
    ISBN: 978-1-4380-0137-1
    1. Commercial correspondence. I. Title.
    HF5721.H43 2013
808.06′6651—dc23   2012037072

9 8 7 6 5 4

Kaplan, Inc., d/b/a Barron's Educational Series print books are available at special quantity discounts to use for sales promotions, employee premiums, or educational purposes. For more information or to purchase books, please call the Simon & Schuster special sales department at 866-506-1949.

Contents

Table of Model Letters

Introduction

Many lessons can be learned during times of economic and financial uncertainty. For readers of this book, a few of these lessons are particularly important. We live in an "IT age," when information is essential. Yet information can also be a problem. If it is incomplete or incoherent, insufficient or unavailable, inaccurate or outright incorrect, information will be very costly, harmful to businesses as well as individuals. And while most information today is communicated electronically, rather than on paper or in conversation, it still consists mainly of numbers and language. This book is concerned with language—using language to communicate information that is complete, correct, comprehensible . . . and valuable.

This brings us to another lesson to be drawn from events in the economy. When jobs are scarce and competition for them is high, skills that apply to a variety of fields become especially valuable. Most essential are the skills that enable a worker to switch careers, adapt to new work environments, and interact with unfamiliar people in unfamiliar situations. High among these skills is the ability to communicate.

Of course, machines are excellent tools for organizing and transmitting information, but people must be able to use that information. A successful businessperson must be able to express information and ideas in clear, comprehensible language, as well as interpret and use information communicated by others. The purpose of *How to Write Better Business Letters* is to help readers add communication skills to their résumés. Our primary focus is on the various categories of business correspondence, with an emphasis on the styles and formats appropriate to each. Because business success also requires mastery of the fundamentals of English, new to this edition is an overview of English grammar, along with a look at the rules for punctuation, capitalization, abbreviation, and the written use of numbers.

Our goal is that, with the help of this book, readers will face opportunities to communicate in business with confidence and appreciation for the value of the written word.

1.
Business Style

Tone

Second to grammatical correctness, achieving an appropriate business style may be the biggest problem for the writer of business letters. A sure sign of an inexperienced writer, in fact, is the obvious attempt to sound too "business-like."

> As per your request, please find enclosed herewith a check in the amount of $16.49.

Such expressions as "herewith" and "as per" contribute nothing to the message while making the letter sound stilted and stiff.

The first step, then, to writing successful business correspondence is to relax. While business letters will vary in tone from familiar to formal, they should all sound natural. Within the limits of standard English, of course, you should try to say things in a "regular" way:

> As you requested, I am enclosing a check for $16.49.

If you resist the temptation to sound businesslike, you will end up being more business-minded. The second version of our sample sentence is not only more personal and friendly, it is also more efficient. It uses fewer words, taking less time to write and prepare as well as to read and comprehend.

With this initial piece of advice in mind, review the following list of words and expressions. Then plan to eliminate these terms from your business writing vocabulary.

EXPRESSIONS TO AVOID IN BUSINESS LETTERS

according to our records
acknowledge receipt of
as to, with reference to, with
  regard to, with respect to
at hand, on hand
attached please find, attached
  hereto, enclosed herewith,
  enclosed please find
beg to inform, beg to tell
duly
for your information
hereby, theretofore, herewith

I have your letter
I wish to thank, may I ask
in due time, in due course of time
in receipt of
in the near future
in view of
our Mrs. _____
permit me to say
pursuant to
thank you again
thank you in advance
thereon

Now review this second list. Plan in your own writing to replace the expressions on the left with those on the right.

Instead of . . .	Use . . .
advise, inform	say, tell, let us know
along these lines, on the order of	like, similar to
as per	as, according to
at an early date, at your earliest convenience	soon, today, next week, *a specific date*
at this time, at the present time at this writing	now, at present
check to cover	check for
deem	believe, consider
due to the fact that, because of the fact that	because
favor, communication	letter, memo, *et al.*
for the purpose of	for
forward	send
free of charge	free
in accordance with	according to
in advance of, prior to	before
in compliance with	as you requested
in re, re	regarding, concerning
in the amount of	for
in the event that	if, in case
kindly	please
of recent date	recent
party	person, *a specific name*
said	*not to be used as an adjective*
same	*not to be used as a noun*
subsequent to	after, since
the writer, the undersigned	I/me
up to this writing	until now

Consider the difference between these two versions of the same letter:

EXAMPLE 1

Dear Mr. Singh:

With reference to your order for a Nashito camcorder, we are in receipt of your check and are returning same.

I beg to inform you that, as a manufacturer, our company sells camcorders to dealers only. In compliance with our wholesale agreement, we deem it best to refrain from direct business with private consumers.

For your information, there are many retailers in your vicinity who carry Nashito camcorders. Attached please find a list of said dealers.

Hoping you understand.

Yours truly,

EXAMPLE 2

Dear Mr. Singh:

We have received your order for a Nashito camcorder but, unfortunately, must return your check.

As a manufacturer, we sell only to dealers, with whom we have very explicit wholesale agreements.

Nevertheless, we sincerely appreciate your interest in Nashito products. We are therefore enclosing a list of retailers in your community who carry a full line of our camcorders. Any one of them will be happy to serve you.

Sincerely yours,

Attitude

While striving for a natural tone, you should also aim for a positive attitude. Even when the subject of your letter is unpleasant, it is important to remain courteous and tactful. Building and sustaining the goodwill of your reader should be an underlying goal of nearly any letter you write. Even a delinquent account may someday become a paying customer.

A simple "please" or "thank you" is often enough to make a mundane letter more courteous. Instead of:

> We have received your order.

you might try:

> Thank you for your recent order.

Or, in place of the impersonal:

> Checking our records, we have verified the error in your November bill.

you could help retain a customer by writing:

> Please accept our sincere apologies for the error in your November bill.

Saying "We are sorry" or "I appreciate" can do much to build rewarding business relations.

On the other hand, you must be tactful when delivering unpleasant messages. **Never** accuse your reader with expressions such as "your error" or "your failure." An antagonistic letter would say:

> Because you have refused to pay your long overdue bill, your credit rating is in jeopardy.

A more diplomatic letter (and therefore one more apt to get results) might say:

> Because the $520 balance on your account is now over ninety days past due, your credit rating is in jeopardy.

Because the second sentence refrains from attacking the reader personally (and also includes important details), it will be read more receptively.

A word of caution is necessary here. Some writers, in an effort to be pleasant, end their letters with sentence fragments:

> Looking forward to your early reply.
> Hoping to hear from you soon.
> Thanking you for your interest.

These participial phrases (note the *-ing* form in each) should **not** be used to conclude a letter. There is never an excuse for grammatical flaws, especially when complete sentences will serve the purpose well:

> We look forward to your early reply.
> I hope to hear from you soon.
> Thank you for your interest.

Consider the difference between these two versions of the same memo:

EXAMPLE 1

TO: Department Supervisors

FROM: Assistant Director

Inform your subordinates:

1. Because so many have taken advantage of past leniency, lateness will no longer be overlooked. Paychecks will be docked as of Monday, March 6.

2. As a result of employee slovenliness, which has required the increased service of an exterminator, any employees caught eating at their work station will be subject to disciplinary action.

As supervisors, you will be required to enforce these new regulations.

EXAMPLE 2

TO: _____

FROM: Wanda Hatch, Assistant Director

Unfortunately, a few people have taken advantage of lenient company policies regarding lateness and personal phone calls. As a result, we must all now conform to tougher regulations.

Please inform the members of your department that:

1. Beginning Monday, March 6, the paychecks of employees who are late will be docked.

2. Eating at our desks will no longer be permitted.

It is a shame that the abuses of a few must cost the rest of us. But we are asking all department supervisors to help us enforce these new rules.

The *"You* Approach"

Courtesy and tact are sometimes achieved by what is called a *you* approach. In other words, your letter should be reader oriented and sound as if you share your reader's point of view. For example:

> Please accept our apologies for the delay.

is perfectly polite. But:

> We hope you have not been seriously inconvenienced by the delay.

lets your reader know that you care.

The *you* approach does **not** mean you should avoid "I" and "we" when necessary. When you do use these pronouns, though, keep a few pointers in mind:

1. Use "I" when you are referring to yourself (or to the person who will actually sign the letter).
2. Use "we" when you are referring to the company itself.
3. Do **not** use the company name or "our company," both of which, like the terms listed earlier in this chapter, sound stilted. This practice is rather like referring to oneself by one's name, rather than "I" or "me."

Also, you should be careful to use your reader's name sparingly in the body of your letter. Although this practice seems, at first glance, to personalize a letter, it can sound condescending.

Now, compare the two letters that follow, and see if you recognize the features that make the second letter more *"you* oriented."

EXAMPLE 1

Dear Ms. Biggs:

Having conducted our standard credit investigation, we have concluded that it would be unwise for us to grant you credit at this time.

We believe that the extent of your current obligations makes you a bad credit risk. As you can understand, it is in our best interest to grant charge accounts only to those customers with proven ability to pay.

Please accept our sincere regrets and feel free to continue to shop at Allen's on a cash basis.

Sincerely yours,

EXAMPLE 2

Dear Miss Biggs:

I am sorry to inform you that your application for an Allen's charge account has been turned down.

Our credit department believes that, because of your current obligations, additional credit might be difficult for you to handle at this time. Your credit reputation is too valuable to be placed in jeopardy. We will be delighted, of course, to reconsider your application in the future should your financial responsibilities be reduced. Until then, we hope you will continue to shop at Allen's where **every** customer is our prime concern.

Sincerely yours,

"Sexist" Language

Once women had assumed a larger and larger role in the workplace, the words used to describe business roles had to be reexamined. Since, for example, a "businessman" often turned out to be a woman, more and more people opted for the sexually neutral term "businessperson."

The third person singular pronouns in English (*he/she*, *him/her*, *his/hers*) are still divided by gender, and so pronoun use continues to present a problem for the writer wishing to avoid "sexist" language. Traditionally, masculine pronouns have been used to refer to abstract, singular human nouns:

> An *employer* must be able to rely on *his* secretary.

But this is no longer considered acceptable.

To avoid the problem, several solutions are possible. A common approach, if an awkward one, is to use both third person singular pronouns:

> An employer must be able to rely on *his* or *her* secretary.

This, however, can become extremely cumbersome, especially when a passage contains several pronouns. Some writers, therefore, revise their sentence to avoid singular human nouns in the first place; that way, a third person plural pronoun (with no gender reference) may be used:

> *Employers* must be able to rely on *their* secretaries.

Yet another way to handle the problem, perhaps the simplest (and the one followed frequently in this book), is to alternate the masculine and feminine pronouns throughout your writing.

Keep in mind, though, that many companies have policies regarding sexist language. Some, for instance, still forbid the use of the term *Ms.* on company correspondence; some retain old forms such as *chairman* or *congressman*. Similarly, a company may have a policy regarding pronoun use; before you revise your boss's or your own letters to eliminate all the "sexist" pronouns, find out where your company stands on the issue.

Organization

One further word about style: a good business letter must be well organized. You must *plan in advance* everything you want to say; you must *say everything necessary* in your message; and then you must stop. In short, a letter must be logical, complete, and concise.

When planning a letter and before you start to write, jot down the main point you want to make. Then, list all the details necessary to make that point; these may be facts, reasons, explanations, etc. Finally, rearrange your list; in the letter, you will want to mention things in a logical order so that your message will come across as clearly as possible.

Making a letter complete takes place during the planning stage, too. Check your list to make sure you have included all the relevant details; the reader of your finished letter must have all the information he or she will need. In addition to facts, reasons, and explanations, necessary information could also entail an appeal to your reader's emotions or understanding. In other words, **say everything you can to elicit from your reader the response you'd like**.

On the other hand, you must be careful not to say too much. You must know when a letter is finished. If a message is brief, resist the temptation to "pad" it; if you've said what you have to say in just a few lines, don't try to fill the letter out. One mistake is to reiterate an idea. If you've already offered your thanks, you will upset the logical order and, therefore, the impact of your letter if you end with:

> Thank you once again.

Tacking on a separate additional message will similarly weaken the effect of your main point. Imagine receiving a collection letter for a long overdue bill that concludes:

> Let us take this opportunity to remind you that our January White Sale
> begins next week, with three preview days for our special charge customers.

Don't, moreover, give your reader more information than is needed:

> Because my husband's birthday is October 12, I would like to order the
> three-piece luggage ensemble in your fall catalog.

Certainly, an order clerk would much prefer to know the style number of the luggage than the date of your husband's birth.

In a similar vein, you should strive to eliminate redundant words and phrases from your letters. For example:

> I have received your invitation *inviting me* to participate in your annual Career
> Conference.

Since all invitations invite, the words "inviting me" are superfluous.
Another common mistake is to say:

> the green-colored carpet

or:

> the carpet that is green in color

Green *is* a color, so to use the word "color" is repetitious.
Adverbs often cause the same problem:

> If we cooperate together, the project will be finished quickly.

Cooperate already means "work together," so using the word "together" is unnecessary.

Also, when one word will accurately replace several, use the one word. Instead of:

> Mr. Kramer handled the job *in an efficient manner*.

say:

> Mr. Kramer handled the job *efficiently*.

The following list of common redundancies should help you eliminate the problem from your writing:

REDUNDANT EXPRESSIONS

Don't Use . . .	*Use . . .*
and et cetera	et cetera
as a result of	because
as otherwise	otherwise
at about	about
attached hereto	attached
at this point in time	at this time; now
avail oneself of	use
be of the opinion	believe
both alike	alike
both together	together
check into	check
connect up	connect
continue on	continue
cooperate together	cooperate
customary practice	practice
during the time that	while
each and every	each *or* every
enclosed herewith	enclosed
enter into	enter
forward by post	mail
free gift	gift
have a tendency to	tend to
in many instances	often
in spite of the fact that	although
in the amount of	for
in the event that	if
in the matter of	about
in the process of being	being
in this day and age	nowadays
inform of the reason	tell why
is of the opinion	believes
letter under date of	letter of
letter with regard to	letter about
new beginner	beginner
on account of the fact that	because
owing to the fact that	because, since
past experience	experience

place emphasis on	emphasize
place an order for	order
repeat again	repeat
same identical	identical
send an answer	reply
up above	above
whether or not	whether
write your name	sign

Now consider the following two sample letters. Notice the redundancies in the first that are eliminated in the second.

EXAMPLE 1

Dear Ms. Rodriguez:

I am very pleased with the invitation that I received from you inviting me to make a speech for the National Association of Veterinarians on June 11. Unfortunately, I regret that I cannot attend the meeting on June 11. I feel that I do not have sufficient time to prepare myself because I received your invitation on June 3 and it is not enough time to prepare myself completely for the speech.

Yours truly,

EXAMPLE 2

Dear Ms. Rodriguez:

I am pleased with the invitation to speak to the National Association of Veterinarians. Unfortunately, I cannot attend the meeting on June 11.

I feel that I will not have sufficient time to prepare myself because I received your invitation on June 3.

I will be happy to address your organization on another occasion if you would give me a bit more notice. Best of luck with your meeting.

Sincerely yours,

Of course, as you exclude irrelevant details and repetitions, you should be careful **not** to cut corners by leaving out necessary words. For example, some writers, in a misguided attempt at efficiency, omit articles (*the*, *a*, and *an*) and prepositions:

Please send order special delivery.

The only effect of omitting "the" and "by" here is to make the request curt and impersonal. The correct sentence is:

Please send the order by special delivery.

> **Note:** Composing directly on your computer can streamline your efforts toward developing a business style. No equipment will compose your message, but you will find it easier to make changes and corrections when you "write" at the screen rather than on paper. On the other hand, because it simplifies the act of revision, word-processing software leaves you no excuse for careless turns of phrase or grammatical errors.

Electronic Mail

E-mail (an electronic message sent via the Internet) is the medium *du jour.* It's faster than the postal service and less expensive than a telephone call. It's more casual than a written letter but less personal than your own voice. Consequently, e-mail is appropriate when immediacy is desirable and informality acceptable.

While any business correspondence can technically (or technologically) be sent via e-mail, not all messages should be. Some are obvious. You surely wouldn't send a message of condolence to a colleague by e-mail. Nor are you likely to e-mail a lengthy report. But nowadays you would probably e-mail coworkers rather than distribute a memo. You would e-mail a brief "update" to clients rather than mail a written announcement. When deciding to use e-mail, you must use your judgment: If the situation is not particularly formal and the message can be kept brief, then e-mail is probably acceptable. If the permanence conveyed by a piece of paper is desired or personal contact would strengthen the business relationship, then don't send e-mail.

We've become so accustomed to conducting personal communications by e-mail that it is important to remember the basic differences between *personal correspondence* and *business correspondence.* Of course, you already know that your tone of voice should be appropriate to the business relationship you have with the person you are e-mailing. But when using the Internet, there are some other important differences to keep in mind.

- Do **not** use "texting" abbreviations (such as BTW for "by the way")—they are annoying and not universally recognized.

- Do **not** use emoticons (such as :) a smiley)—they are frivolous and make your message seem silly.

- Do **not** use all capital letters—this signifies "shouting" and will be perceived as offensive.

- Do **not** "flame" (that is, express outrage)—this will be viewed as rude and unbusinesslike.

- Do **not** use a cute or clever signature (such as BUILT2LAST)—this is adolescent, and your own name would be much more professional.

Remember a very important difference between *e-mail* and *written mail*: **e-mail is not private**, especially at work. Not only is e-mail stored on disk; at a corporation it is routinely backed up. E-mail can be forwarded to others and, with the slightest error in the Internet address, may be sent to the wrong party. It can, as well, be printed and passed around. For these reasons (not to mention hackers and other security issues), business e-mail must be **discreet**:

- Do **not** express criticism of a third party.
- Do **not** reprimand your recipient.
- Do **not** convey confidential, classified, or restricted information.

Just keep in mind: **Never send by e-mail a message that you would not want others to see.**

E-mail Format

Format will be dictated by your ISP (Internet Service Provider) but will invariably have boxes for you to fill in. (See Figure 1-1.)

- SEND TO
  Enter the recipient's Internet address.

- COPY TO
  Enter the addresses of additional people, if any, you'd like to receive the message.

- SUBJECT
  Enter a brief, simple, informative subject line. Be careful not to sound like spam (junk e-mail). E-mail with a heading such as "Look at this!!" may be deleted without being read.

- MESSAGE
  Enter the text of your message. (Be sure that if you've composed your text in a word-processing program, it will be formatted legibly when you convert to e-mail.)

  Note: To e-mail an already existing document, display the document on your screen and click "File" and then, on the drop-down menu, click "send as," and then choose the appropriate action.

- ATTACHMENTS
  Click "Attachments" to send material from a file *with* the e-mail rather than as part of the text. In addition to documents and programs, this may include pictures from an image file, sounds from an audio file, movies from a video file, and so on. Keep in mind: (1) because attachments may contain a virus, most people won't download them if they don't know you or aren't expecting the e-mail; (2) the attachments must be done with a program your recipient can handle; (3) as with the **text**, if you use material from a word-processing program, the e-mail may have program defaults that make the attachment incomprehensible.

Basically, an e-mail message resembles a memo and, like a memo, should be kept brief. But don't sacrifice professionalism for brevity. If you need to attach a file and it would be convenient for your recipient, do so. Just remember the basic principles: Be **complete**, **concise**, and **correct**. Say everything you need to say, say nothing unnecessary, and say it all in grammatically correct form. Be sure, also, to include contact information beyond just your own e-mail address. Include your telephone and fax numbers so your recipient has multiple ways to respond.

Receiving E-mail

When you receive e-mail, you have several options. If it looks like spam, of course, you can **delete** it. If the subject line and sender sound legitimate, you can **read** it and then delete it. If the message is important enough to **save**, you can:

- save it in a "folder" (a file of messages);
- save it in a regular file;
- print it and retain the paper copy.

To **reply** to e-mail, there are two bits of advice:

- Be sure to fill in the **send to** box correctly.
- Incorporate part of the original message in the text of your response as a courtesy to refresh your recipient's memory.

You can also **forward** e-mail by incorporating a message you receive into a new message you send to someone else. A **business ethics warning**: do not forward e-mail you reasonably think the sender expected would remain confidential. Plus, if you do forward the text, or part of the text, be sure you don't distort the original meaning when you put it into your own new context.

It is also possible to **redirect** e-mail. If you receive, in error, e-mail meant for someone else, you can forward it (also called "bouncing" or "remailing") to the correct party, with or without a note of explanation.

Finally, be sure to **check** your e-mail regularly. The main point of e-mail is **speed**!

A Word of Caution

Do **not** send or receive personal e-mail at work. (Neither should you surf the Web or shop online.) Besides the fact that using your company's computer for personal tasks is inappropriate and unprofessional, it can also cost you your job. Remember, **e-mail is *not* private**. It can be monitored. It is stored. And it can be used against you at any time.

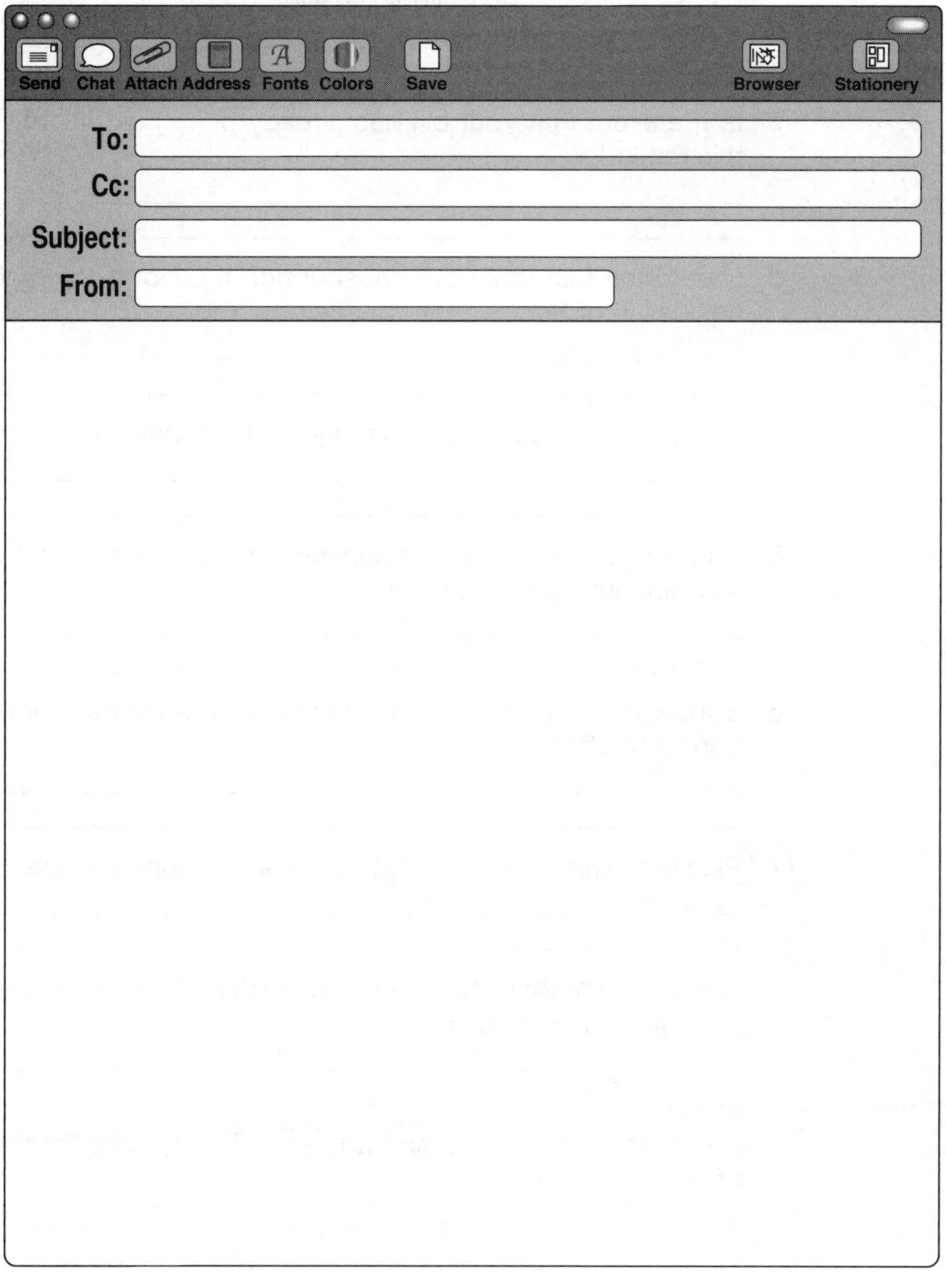

Figure 1–1
E-mail Format

■■■■■ PRACTICE CORRESPONDENCE

A. *In the space provided, rewrite each sentence to eliminate the stilted tone.*

Example:
We are in receipt of your letter dated December 13, 20—.
We have received your letter of December 13, 20—.

1. Please advise us as to your decision.

   _____

   _____

2. In the event that your bill has already been paid, kindly disregard this reminder.

   _____

   _____

3. Due to the fact that your subscription has not been renewed, the next issue of *Run!* will be your last.

   _____

   _____

4. Feel free to contact the undersigned if you have any questions.

   _____

   _____

5. Pursuant to our telephone conversation of Friday last, I would like to verify our agreement.

   _____

   _____

6. Subsequent to last month's meeting, several new policies have gone into effect.

   _____

   _____

7. Please forward your order at your earliest convenience.

   _____

   _____

8. Our deluxe model copier is on the order of a Rolls Royce in terms of quality and precision.

   _____

   _____

9. Enclosed please find a self-addressed reply card for the purpose of your convenience.

   _____

   _____

10. I beg to inform you that, despite your impressive background, we feel that your skills do not quite match our needs.

    _____

    _____

B. *In the space provided, replace each expression with one or two words that convey the same meaning.*

1. prepare a copy of your hard drive on tape or disk

    _____

2. a shopkeeper with a good reputation

    _____

3. performed the work with great effect

    _____

4. a sharp rise in prices accompanied by a fall in the value of currency

    _____

5. some time in the near future

    _____

6. ran off several copies of the original on a duplicating machine

    _____

7. people with the responsibility of managing an office

    _____

8. suffering from fatique

    _____

9. in a decisive way

    _____

10. handwriting that is nearly impossible to read

    _____

C. *On another sheet of paper, rewrite these letters to make them more courteous, concise, and "you-oriented."*

Dear Ms. Lawson:

I regret to inform you that we are completely booked up for the week of August 22. We have no rooms available because the National Audiologists Association will be holding its convention at our hotel during the week of August 22. As you will surely understand, we have to reserve as many rooms as possible for members of the association.

If you can't change the date of your trip, maybe you could find the double room with bath that you want at another hotel here in Little Rock.

Cordially,

_____

Dear Mr. Ross:

With reference to your letter of Thursday last, I can't answer it because my boss, Ms. Leonard, is out of town. If I gave you any information about the new contract with Hastings Development Corporation, she might not like it.

If Ms. Leonard wants you to have that information, I'll have her write to you when she returns in two weeks.

Yours truly,

———————————————

Dear Ms. Graham:

The information you want having to do with filing for an absentee ballot for the upcoming presidential election, is not available from our office.

Why don't you write your local Board of Elections?

Sorry.

Sincerely yours,

2.
Letter Format

Before we begin to discuss letter *content*, we must examine letter appearance because the physical condition of a letter makes the first impression on your reader. Before reading even one word you have written, the reader has formed an opinion based on the way your letter looks—the arrangement, the print quality, etc.

When you have composed the body of your letter and are ready to print, keep in mind three things:

Printing Letters should be single spaced with double spacing between paragraphs. Print should be clear and dark. Errors should not be erased or corrected after printing.

Paragraphing Paragraph breaks should come at logical points in your message and should also result in an EVEN appearance. A one-line paragraph followed by an eight-line paragraph will look bottom heavy. Paragraphs of *approximately* the same length will please the eye.

White space In addition to the space created by paragraphing, leave space by centering the body of your letter on the page. An ample margin of white space should surround the message, top and bottom as well as both sides. If a letter is brief, avoid beginning to print too high on the page; if a letter is long, do not hesitate to use an additional sheet of paper. (See Figure 2–1 for recommended spacing between letter parts.)

> **Note:** Although preparing your letter on a computer will facilitate the job of formatting, you still control the organization of your message and remain ultimately responsible for the final appearance of your letter.

Parts of a Business Letter

While the horizontal placement of letter parts may vary (see the next section, "Arrangement Styles"), the vertical order of these parts is standard. Refer to the model letter (Figure 2–1) as you study the following list of letter parts.

1. LETTERHEAD: This, of course, is printed and supplied by your employer. It is used only for the first page of a letter.
2. DATELINE: The date on which the letter is being prepared appears a few lines below the letterhead.
3. INSIDE ADDRESS: The address of your reader is printed as it will appear on the envelope.

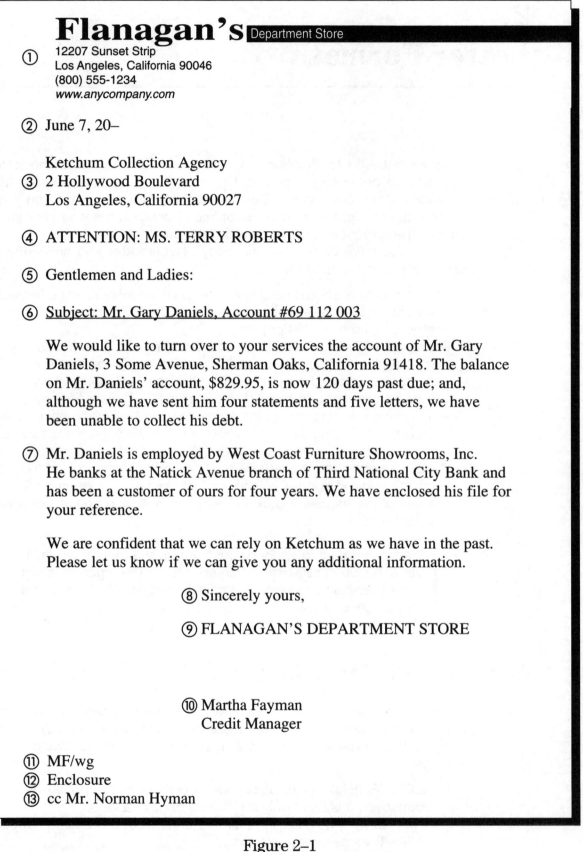

① **Flanagan's** Department Store
12207 Sunset Strip
Los Angeles, California 90046
(800) 555-1234
www.anycompany.com

② June 7, 20–

Ketchum Collection Agency
③ 2 Hollywood Boulevard
Los Angeles, California 90027

④ ATTENTION: MS. TERRY ROBERTS

⑤ Gentlemen and Ladies:

⑥ Subject: Mr. Gary Daniels, Account #69 112 003

We would like to turn over to your services the account of Mr. Gary Daniels, 3 Some Avenue, Sherman Oaks, California 91418. The balance on Mr. Daniels' account, $829.95, is now 120 days past due; and, although we have sent him four statements and five letters, we have been unable to collect his debt.

⑦ Mr. Daniels is employed by West Coast Furniture Showrooms, Inc. He banks at the Natick Avenue branch of Third National City Bank and has been a customer of ours for four years. We have enclosed his file for your reference.

We are confident that we can rely on Ketchum as we have in the past. Please let us know if we can give you any additional information.

⑧ Sincerely yours,

⑨ FLANAGAN'S DEPARTMENT STORE

⑩ Martha Fayman
Credit Manager

⑪ MF/wg
⑫ Enclosure
⑬ cc Mr. Norman Hyman

Figure 2–1
The Parts of a Business Letter

4. ATTENTION LINE: This is not always required. It should be used when the letter is addressed to a company, organization, or department as a whole, but you want it to be handled by a specific individual within that unit. It should be underlined or printed in capitals.

5. SALUTATION: While "Dear Sir," "Dear Madam," "Dear Madam or Sir," "Gentlemen," "Gentlemen and Ladies" are acceptable in cases of extreme formality, you should otherwise use an individual's name whenever it is known. When the reader's name is *not* known, the person's title is the next best term in a salutation.

6. SUBJECT LINE: Like the attention line, this is often omitted, but its inclusion is a courtesy to your readers. By alerting them to the content of your message, you enable them to decide whether the letter requires immediate attention. It should be underlined or printed in capitals.

7. BODY: This is the actual message of your letter.

8. COMPLIMENTARY CLOSING: This is a polite, formal way to end a letter; standard forms are "Yours truly" or "Truly yours," "Sincerely yours," "Respectfully yours," etc. Excessively familiar closings should be avoided, except in special situations. "Best wishes," for example, could be used when the reader is well known to you. Expressions such as "Fondly" or "Love," should, obviously, be reserved for private correspondence.

9. COMPANY SIGNATURE: Another item often omitted from less formal correspondence, it should be used when the signer of the letter is writing as a spokesperson for the company, not as an individual. Since this information appears in the letterhead, some companies omit it altogether.

10. SIGNER'S IDENTIFICATION: Printed four lines below the previous item to allow space for the signature, this includes the signer's name and any relevant titles.

11. REFERENCE INITIALS: Consisting of the signer's initials in capitals followed by a slash or colon followed by the lowercase initials of the person preparing the letter, this item serves as a reminder of who prepared the letter.

12. ENCLOSURE REMINDER: Consisting of the word "enclosure" (or "enc" or "encl"), or the word "enclosure" followed by a list of the enclosed items, this is a practical courtesy to prevent your reader from discarding important matter with the envelope.

13. "CC" NOTATION: Also a courtesy, this tells the reader who has been sent a copy of the letter.

Arrangement Styles

As previously noted, the horizontal placement of letter parts is flexible—within the limits of five basic styles. Often, however, a company will have a preferred arrangement style that employees are required to use.

FULL-BLOCKED (Figure 2–2): All letter parts begin at the left margin. It is therefore the fastest traditional arrangement style to prepare.

NORP

NATIONAL ORGANIZATION OF RETIRED PERSONS
123 Main Street, Freeport, Vermont 66622
800-555-1234 *www.anycompany.com*

October 14, 20–

Ms. Iva Stravinsky
Attorney-at-Law
2 Maple Street
Freeport, Vermont 66622

Dear Ms. Stravinsky

Subject: Guest Lecture

The members of the Freeport chapter of the National Organization of Retired Persons would indeed be interested in a lecture on "Recent Changes in the Financing of Medicare." Therefore, with much appreciation, I accept your offer to address our club.

The NORP meets every Tuesday at 8 P.M. in the auditorium of Freeport High School. The programs for our meetings through November 20 have already been established. However, I will call you in a few days to schedule a date for your lecture for the first Tuesday after the 20th that meets your convenience.

The membership and I look forward to your lecture on a topic so important to us all.

Sincerely yours

NATIONAL ORGANIZATION OF RETIRED PERSONS

Henry Purcell
President

HP/bm

Figure 2–2
Full-Blocked Letter Style

BLOCKED (Figure 2–3): Like full-blocked, all letter parts begin at the left margin, *except* the dateline, complimentary closing, company signature, and writer's identification, which start at the horizontal center of the page. (Options—the dateline may end at the right margin; attention and subject lines may be centered or indented five or ten spaces.)

SEMI-BLOCKED *or* MODIFIED BLOCKED (Figure 2–4): This is the same as a blocked letter with one change: the beginning of each paragraph is indented five or ten spaces.

SQUARE-BLOCKED (Figure 2–5): This is the same as a full-blocked letter with two changes: the date appears on the same line as the start of the inside address and ends at the right margin; reference initials and enclosure reminder appear on the same lines as the signature and signer's identification. As a result, corners are squared off. This arrangement saves space, allowing longer letters to fit onto a single page. (Be sure to use a line at least 50 spaces long so that the inside address won't run into the dateline.)

SIMPLIFIED *or* AMS (Figure 2–6): Designed by the Administrative Management Society, this style is the same as full-blocked, except: (1) no salutation or complimentary closing is used; (2) an entirely capitalized subject line (without the word "subject") *must* be used; (3) the signer's identification is printed in all capitals; and (4) lists are indented five spaces unless numbered or lettered (in which case they are blocked with no periods after the numbers or letters). This style is extremely efficient, requiring much less time to prepare than other styles. However, it is also impersonal. For this reason, the reader's name should be mentioned at least once in the body.

Punctuation Styles

Regardless of punctuation style, the *only* letter parts (outside of the body) to be followed by punctuation marks are the salutation and complimentary closing. Within the body, the general rules of punctuation apply.

OPEN: No punctuation is used, except in the body. (See Figure 2–2.)

STANDARD: The salutation is followed by a colon; the complimentary closing is followed by a comma. (See Figure 2–3.)

> **Note:** The salutation and closing should be punctuated consistently: either *both* are followed by punctuation or *neither* is followed by punctuation. Note, too, that a comma is NOT used after the salutation; this practice is reserved for private correspondence.

NORP

NATIONAL ORGANIZATION OF RETIRED PERSONS
123 Main Street, Freeport, Vermont 66622
800-555-1234 *www.anycompany.com*

October 14, 20–

Ms. Iva Stravinsky
Attorney-at-Law
2 Maple Street
Freeport, Vermont 66622

Dear Ms. Stravinsky:

Subject: Guest Lecture

The members of the Freeport chapter of the National Organization of Retired Persons would indeed be interested in a lecture on "Recent Changes in the Financing of Medicare." Therefore, with much appreciation, I accept your offer to address our club.

The NORP meets every Tuesday at 8 P.M. in the auditorium of Freeport High School. The programs for our meetings through November 20 have already been established. However, I will call you in a few days to schedule a date for your lecture for the first Tuesday after the 20th that meets your convenience.

The membership and I look forward to your lecture on a topic so important to us all.

Sincerely yours,

Henry Purcell
President

HP/bm

Figure 2–3
Blocked Letter Style

NATIONAL ORGANIZATION OF RETIRED PERSONS
123 Main Street, Freeport, Vermont 66622
800-555-1234 *www.anycompany.com*

October 14, 20–

Ms. Iva Stravinsky
Attorney-at-Law
2 Maple Street
Freeport, Vermont 66622

Dear Ms. Stravinsky:

<u>Subject: Guest Lecture</u>

The members of the Freeport chapter of the National Organization of Retired Persons would indeed be interested in a lecture on "Recent Changes in the Financing of Medicare." Therefore, with much appreciation, I accept your offer to address our club.

The NORP meets every Tuesday at 8 P.M. in the auditorium of Freeport High School. The programs for our meetings through November 20 have already been established. However, I will call you in a few days to schedule a date for your lecture for the first Tuesday after the 20th that meets your convenience.

The membership and I look forward to your lecture on a topic so important to us all.

Sincerely yours,

Henry Purcell
President

HP/bm

Figure 2–4
Semi-Blocked Letter Style

NORP

NATIONAL ORGANIZATION OF RETIRED PERSONS
123 Main Street, Freeport, Vermont 66622
800-555-1234 *www.anycompany.com*

Ms. Iva Stravinsky   October 14, 20–
Attorney-at-Law
2 Maple Street
Freeport, Vermont 66622

Dear Ms. Stravinsky:

SUBJECT: GUEST LECTURE

The members of the Freeport chapter of the National Organization
of Retired Persons would indeed be interested in a lecture on "Recent
Changes in the Financing of Medicare." Therefore, with much appreciation,
I accept your offer to address our club.

The NORP meets every Tuesday at 8 P.M. in the auditorium of Freeport
High School. The programs for our meetings through November 20 have
already been established. However, I will call you in a few days to schedule
a date for your lecture for the first Tuesday after the 20th that meets your
convenience.

The membership and I look forward to your lecture on a topic so important to
us all.

Sincerely yours,

NATIONAL ORGANIZATION OF RETIRED PERSONS

Henry Purcell
President   HP/bm

Figure 2–5
Square-Blocked Letter Style

NATIONAL ORGANIZATION OF RETIRED PERSONS
123 Main Street, Freeport, Vermont 66622
800-555-1234 *www.anycompany.com*

October 14, 20–

Ms. Iva Stravinsky
Attorney-at-Law
2 Maple Street
Freeport, Vermont 66622

GUEST LECTURE

The members of the Freeport chapter of the National Organization of Retired Persons would indeed be interested in a lecture on "Recent Changes in the Financing of Medicare." Therefore, with much appreciation, I accept your offer to address our club.

The NORP meets every Tuesday at 8 P.M. in the auditorium of Freeport High School. The programs for our meetings through November 20 have already been established. However, I will call you in a few days to schedule a date for your lecture for the first Tuesday after the 20th that meets your convenience.

The membership and I look forward, Ms. Stravinsky, to your lecture on a topic so important to us all.

HENRY PURCELL, PRESIDENT

HP/bm

Figure 2–6
Simplified Letter Style

Postscripts

It is best to avoid postscripts; when a letter is well planned, all pertinent information will be included in the body. However, when a postscript is required, it is arranged as the other paragraphs in the letter have been, preceded by "P.S." or "PS":

> P.S. Let me remind you of our special discount on orders for a dozen or more of the same model appliance.

Special Paragraphing

When a message contains quotations of prices or notations of special data, this information is set in a special paragraph (see Figure 2–7), indented five spaces on the left and right, preceded and followed by a blank line.

The Envelope

An envelope should be addressed to correspond with the inside address. On an envelope, though, the state name should be abbreviated in accordance with the United States Postal Service ZIP-code style. On a standard business-size envelope, the address should begin four inches from the left edge, fourteen lines from the top (see Figure 2–8).

In accordance with Postal Service guidelines, the address should be blocked and single-spaced, and should include the ZIP code one space after the state. Because NO information should appear below the ZIP code, special instructions (such as *ATT: Mr. Smith* or *Please Forward*) should be placed four lines below the return address. Similarly, mailing services, such as *Priority Mail* or *Certified Mail*, should be placed below the stamp.

The return address, matching the letterhead, is usually printed on business envelopes.

Facsimiles

Time constraints may require transmitting a letter by facsimile rather than sending it through the mail. When information is needed quickly, it can be requested and subsequently provided promptly by fax, enabling business to continue without delay. Any letter prepared in a standard format certainly may be faxed, but it is customary to precede the letter with a cover sheet. This cover sheet (Figure 2–9) resembles the heading for a memo (see Chapter 10) and contains specific data:

1. the recipient's name, company name, and fax number;
2. the sender's name, company name (if this does not appear in a letterhead) and fax number;

FRANKLIN AND GORDON OFFICE SUPPLIES, INC.
345 Queens Boulevard, Rego Park, New York 11374
(800) 555-1234 www.anycompany.com

September 15, 20–

Robert Nathan, CPA
2 Bourbon Street
New Orleans, Louisiana 70130

Dear Mr. Nathan:

We appreciate your interest in Franklin and Gordon office supplies and are delighted to send you the information you requested:

> Ruled ledger paper, by the ream only, costs $95; with the purchase of six or more reams, the price is reduced to $92 per ream, a savings of at least $18.

> Black, reinforced ledger binders are $55 each; with the purchase of six or more binders, the price is only $53 each, a savings of at least $12.

Because we are the manufacturers of many other fine office supplies, ranging from ball-point pens to promotional novelties, we have enclosed for your consideration a copy of our current catalog. Should you decide to place an order, you may use the convenient order form in the center of the catalog, call our 24-hour toll free number, or order online.

Please let us know if we may be of further assistance.

Sincerely yours,

FRANKLIN AND GORDON OFFICE SUPPLIES, INC.

George Gillian
Customer Service Manager

GG: jc
Enclosure

Figure 2–7
Special Paragraphing

Flanagan's Department Store
12207 Sunset Strip
Los Angeles, California 90046

Attention Ms. Terry Roberts   Registered Mail

Ketchum Collection Agency
2 Hollywood Boulevard
Los Angeles, CA 90027

Figure 2–8
The Envelope

Flanagan's

12207 Sunset Strip

Los Angeles, CA 90046

Tel.(800)555-1234

FAX (555)123-4567

FACSIMILE TRANSMITTAL

TO: _____

COMPANY: _____

FAX NO.: _____

FROM: _____

DATE: _____

TOTAL NUMBER OF PAGES INCLUDING COVER: _____

COMMENTS: _____

_____

_____

Figure 2–9
Facsimile Cover Sheet

3. the date;
4. the total number of pages (including the cover sheet) being faxed;
5. a subject line or a space in which to briefly identify the contents of the fax.

Remember: Since a fax machine is generally used by more than one member of an organization, it is not an appropriate way to send confidential or sensitive documents. If you want your letter read only by your intended recipient, mail it!

PRACTICE CORRESPONDENCE

Prepare this letter in each of the five arrangement styles: (A) Full-blocked, (B) Blocked, (C) Semi-blocked, (D) Square-blocked, and (E) Simplified.

Dateline: July 9, 20—
Inside Address: The Middle Atlantic Institute of Technology,
            1568 Main Street, Danbury, Connecticut 06810
Attention Line: Attention Dean Claude Monet
Salutation: Gentlemen and Ladies
Subject Line: Educational Exchange
Body:

The Commission for Educational Exchange between the United States and Belgium has advised me to contact you in order to obtain employment assistance.

I received my Doctor's Degree with a "grande distinction" from the University of Brussels and would like to teach French (my native language), English, Dutch, or German.

My special field is English literature; I wrote my dissertation on James Joyce, but I am also qualified to teach languages to business students. I have been active in the field of applied linguistics for the past two years at the University of Brussels.

I look forward to hearing from you.
Complimentary Closing: Respectfully yours
Signer's Identification: Jacqueline Brauer
Reference Initials: JB:db

3.
Request Letters

As a businessperson, you will inevitably have to write many request letters. The need for information or special favors, services, or products arises daily in almost every type of business. The reasons for writing a request letter are diverse:

1. to obtain information (such as prices or technical data);
2. to receive printed matter (such as booklets, catalogs, price lists, and reports);
3. to receive sample products;
4. to order merchandise;
5. to engage services (including repair or maintenance services);
6. to make reservations (at hotels, restaurants, theaters);
7. to seek special favors (such as permission, assistance, or advice).

While certain requests, such as ordering merchandise, are routine matters, the general guidelines for business letter writing are especially important when writing any request. Tact and courtesy are essential when you want your readers to *act*. If you want them to act *promptly*, your letter must encourage them to do so.Therefore, all requests should:

1. be specific and brief;
2. be reasonable;
3. provide complete, accurate information.

Inquiries

Usually, an inquiry offers the recipient no immediate reward or advantage beyond the prospect of a future customer or the maintenance of goodwill. Therefore, your inquiry must be worded in such a way that the recipient will respond despite a busy schedule. To do this, you must make your inquiry *easy to answer*.

First of all, you should decide exactly what you want *before* you write. This should include the specific information that you need as well as the course of action you would like your reader to take. Consider this request:

EXAMPLE

Dear Sir or Madam:

Please send us information about your multifunction laser printers so that we will know whether one would be suited to our type of business.

Yours truly,

The recipient of this letter would not know how to respond. She could simply send a brochure or catalog, but she could not possibly explain the advantages of her company's machines without knowing your company's needs. You have *not* made it easy for her to act.

Such an inquiry should include specific questions worded to elicit specific facts. Since the manufacturer of laser printers may make dozens of models, the inquiry should narrow down the type your company would consider.

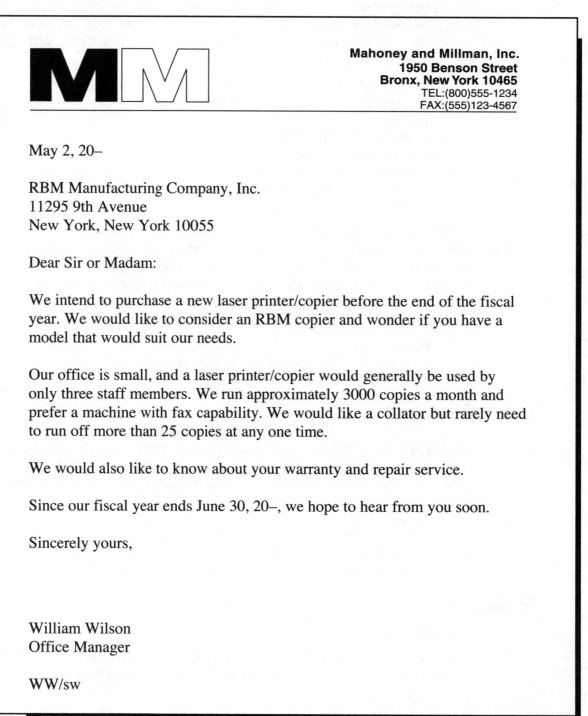

Mahoney and Millman, Inc.
1950 Benson Street
Bronx, New York 10465
TEL:(800)555-1234
FAX:(555)123-4567

May 2, 20–

RBM Manufacturing Company, Inc.
11295 9th Avenue
New York, New York 10055

Dear Sir or Madam:

We intend to purchase a new laser printer/copier before the end of the fiscal year. We would like to consider an RBM copier and wonder if you have a model that would suit our needs.

Our office is small, and a laser printer/copier would generally be used by only three staff members. We run approximately 3000 copies a month and prefer a machine with fax capability. We would like a collator but rarely need to run off more than 25 copies at any one time.

We would also like to know about your warranty and repair service.

Since our fiscal year ends June 30, 20–, we hope to hear from you soon.

Sincerely yours,

William Wilson
Office Manager

WW/sw

Figure 3–1
Inquiry

Notice how the revised letter (Figure 3–1) makes it easier for your reader to respond. You have given a clear picture of what you're looking for, so she can determine which of the company's products might interest you. Moreover, by mentioning the **reason** for your inquiry, you motivate her response. (Your intended purchase is a real potential sale for RBM.) Finally, by letting her know **when** you intend to buy, you've encouraged her to reply promptly.

When a request does *not* hold the prospect for a potential sale, you should make your letter even more convenient for your reader:

1. itemize and list the specific facts you want;
2. enclose a self-addressed, stamped envelope;
3. suggest a way in which you can reciprocate.

EXAMPLE

Dear Mr. Greenbaum:

I am taking a course in Principles of Advertising at Smithville Community College in Smithville, Ohio, and am doing my term project on the ways in which American automobile manufacturers have been competing in the small-car market.

I would therefore greatly appreciate your sending me the following specifications on the new RX-7:

1. Fuel economy statistics

2. Technological advances (such as steering system, brake system, and engine capacity)

3. Available options

I would also find it very helpful if you told me in which magazine (or other mass media) you began your advertising campaign.

I am certain my classmates will find this information extremely interesting. I will be sure to send you a copy of my report as soon as it is complete.

Respectfully yours,

Orders

Many companies use special forms for ordering merchandise or service. They may use their own, called a *purchase order*, or one provided by the seller, called an *order form*. These forms have blank spaces to ensure the inclusion of all necessary information. Their advantage is that they enable a company to number and track all expenditures.

Nevertheless, there will be times when an order must be put into letter format. At such times, you must be sure to include **complete**, **accurate information** because incomplete orders result in delayed deliveries, and inaccurate facts result in receipt of the wrong merchandise.

Every order should include:

1. the name of the item being ordered;
2. the item's number (catalog number, style number, model number, etc.);
3. quantity desired (often in large units such as dozens, cases, reams, etc.);
4. description (such as size, weight, color, material, finish, extra features);
5. unit price;
6. applicable discounts;
7. applicable sales tax;
8. total price;
9. method of payment (such as charge account, including the account number, c.o.d., check, etc.);
10. desired delivery date;
11. method of shipment (such as parcel post or air express);
12. delivery address (which may vary from the billing address);
13. authorized signature.

In addition, if your order is in response to an advertisement, you should mention the source (such as the title and issue date of a magazine or newspaper).

The following letter would run into trouble:

EXAMPLE

Dear Sirs:

Please send me one of your document shredders that I saw advertised for $79.99. I am in the process of eliminating my paper files and could certainly also make use of the free box of fifty shredder bags.

My check is enclosed.

Sincerely,

First of all, an order clerk would not know what to send this customer unless the company manufactured only one document shredder for $79.99. Moreover, instead of providing the **necessary facts**, the writer included unnecessary details. Generally, it is **not necessary to mention a reason for an order**. Orders are routine and handled in quantity; as long as you are a paying customer, your motive for buying does not interest the seller.

While the preceding letter would require interim correspondence before the order could be shipped, the letter in Figure 3–2 would elicit prompt delivery.

627 Seventh Street West
Boise, Idaho 88811
February 14, 20—

National Office Supply, Inc.
2 Commerce Street
Jackson, Mississippi 70707

ATTENTION: SALES DEPARTMENT

Dear Sirs:

I have seen your advertisement in *Office Manager Monthly*, February 20—, and would like to order the following document shredder:

Model P-99C Cross-cut shredder, 5-gallon bin, $79.99

Please also send me a free 50-count box of shredder bags, as offered in your advertisement.

Send my order to the above address by parcel post and charge it, with any applicable sales tax and handling costs, to my VISA account (no. 003 BA22 11CD/ expiration date 3/1/—).

Yours truly,

Edoardo Martinez

Figure 3–2
Order

PRACTICE CORRESPONDENCE

For each of the following activities, prepare a request letter using appropriate arrangement and punctuation styles.

A. You are the program chairperson of the Harrisburg Civic Association. Write a letter to Margaret Belmont, mayor of Harrisburg, asking if she would be willing to attend a future meeting of the association and address the members on a topic of general interest. Meetings are held the second Wednesday of every month at 7:30 P.M. in the basement meeting room of the community center. Previous speakers have included Hiroko Kamata, president of Grand Northern Motels,

Inc., who spoke on the topic "Increasing Tourism in Harrisburg," and Gregory Lardas, CPA, who spoke on the topic "Local Property Tax: Boost or Burden?" You may explain that meetings are attended by approximately 75 community-minded people and that the lecture segment of the meeting usually lasts about one hour.

B. As assistant buyer for Fenway's Toy Store, 1704 North Broadway, Richmond, Virginia 23261, write a letter to the Marco Toy Company, Inc., 223 Sunrise Highway, Glen Cove, New York 11566, to order two dozen Baby Jenny dolls (at $10 each), one dozen Baby Jenny layette sets (at $15 each), and three dozen 18-inch Tootsie-Wootsie teddy bears (at $7 each). You would like to have these items in stock in time for the pre-Christmas selling season. You want to make this purchase on account and have it shipped air express. If Marco has available any special Christmas displays for their merchandise, you would like to receive these, too.

C. As assistant finance manager of your company, it is your responsibility to report to your supervisors about year-end tax-saving measures that can be taken within the organization. Write a letter to Wilda Stewart (Stewart and Stewart CPA's, 466 Main Street, Eugene, Oregon 84403), an accountant you met recently at a seminar on the new federal tax laws. Ask her for information for your report, including pointers on deferring income and accelerating deductions as well as year-end expenditures.

D. Answer the following advertisement in the current issue of *Office Workers' Weekly:*

HANDCRAFTED NETBOOK SLEEVE

Protect your netbook and make a unique fashion statement . . . luxurious calfskin, hand-stitched with asymetrical zippers for vertical or horizontal opening . . . USA sewn from Italian leather . . . choose black, tobacco, or red. $85 plus $7.95 shipping (Iowa residents, please add appropriate sales tax). HNS, Inc., Box 1234, Ames, Iowa 33333.

E. You are a sales supervisor at the Am-Lux Company, Inc., 529 Eaton Avenue, Bethlehem, Pennsylvania 18115. You recently read an article by Louisa Sanchez entitled "From Lead to Deal: Ten Overlooked Steps to Closure" in *High Commission* magazine. You believe the twenty-five salespeople in your department would benefit from reading the article. Write a letter to Ms. Sanchez, in care of *High Commission*, 705 Tenth Avenue, New York, New York 10077, requesting her permission to make twenty-five copies of her article for circulation only within your company.

4.
Replies

A large part of handling a company's correspondence involves **answering** the mail. The ability to phrase an appropriate response is, therefore, a valuable and marketable skill.

Letters of response fall into a number of categories, including:

1. acknowledgments
2. follow-ups
3. confirmations
4. remittances
5. order acknowledgments
6. stopgap letters
7. inquiry replies
8. referrals
9. refusals

Many companies use form letters for certain types of replies, such as order acknowledgments. Nevertheless, a reply is often a fertile sales opportunity, and a personal, carefully worded letter can reap both profits and goodwill.

Like a request, a reply should be *specific* and *complete*. However, a reply need not be brief. Indeed, because a reply must be both *helpful* and *sales oriented*, brevity is often impossible to achieve.

On the other hand, it is essential that a reply be *prompt*. In striving for a *you* approach, this promptness may even be pointed out to the reader:

EXAMPLE

Dear Mr. Mechanic:

I received your letter this morning and wanted to be sure you would have our current price list before the end of the week. . . .

Without patting yourself on the back, such an opening lets your reader know you are *interested* and want to be *helpful*. In fact, whenever possible, a response should go a little further than the original request. An extra bit of information or unasked-for help can turn an inquirer into a steady customer.

Acknowledgments

An acknowledgment (Figure 4–1) should be written when you receive merchandise, material, money, or information. Such a letter is a courtesy, letting your reader know that his mailing or shipment has reached its destination. When the matter received was not an order, an acknowledgment can also serve as a thank-you note.

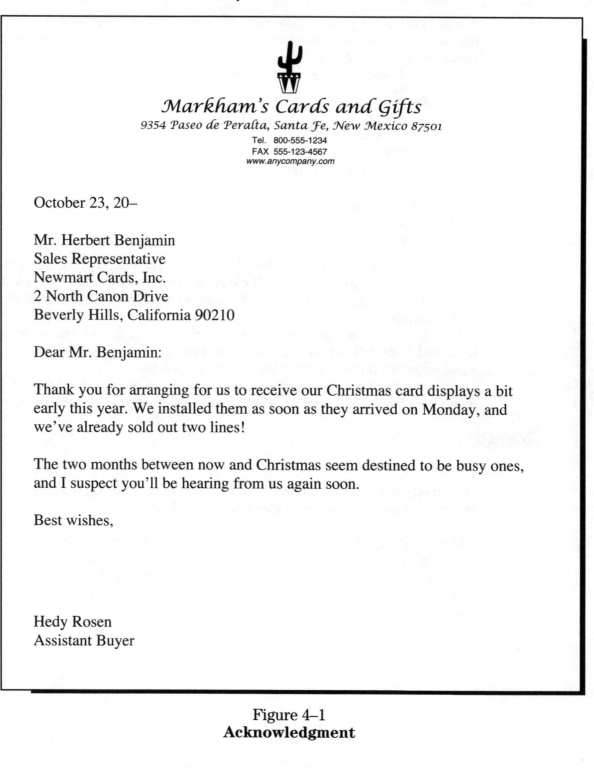

Markham's Cards and Gifts
9354 Paseo de Peralta, Santa Fe, New Mexico 87501
Tel. 800-555-1234
FAX 555-123-4567
www.anycompany.com

October 23, 20–

Mr. Herbert Benjamin
Sales Representative
Newmart Cards, Inc.
2 North Canon Drive
Beverly Hills, California 90210

Dear Mr. Benjamin:

Thank you for arranging for us to receive our Christmas card displays a bit early this year. We installed them as soon as they arrived on Monday, and we've already sold out two lines!

The two months between now and Christmas seem destined to be busy ones, and I suspect you'll be hearing from us again soon.

Best wishes,

Hedy Rosen
Assistant Buyer

Figure 4–1
Acknowledgment

Follow-Ups

After a decision or agreement has been made, either at a meeting or in conversation, it is wise to send a follow-up letter (Figure 4–2) to establish a written record of the transaction.

THE COMMITTEE TO KEEP MINNESOTA GREEN
1023 MAIN STREET, BLACKDUCK, MINNESOTA 56630
(800) 555-1234

June 3, 20–

Ms. Christine Solars
Solars, Solars, and Wright
62 Onigum Road
Walker, Minnesota 56484

Dear Ms. Solars:

We are pleased that you will be participating in the Ecology Colloquium sponsored by the Committee to Keep Minnesota Green. As we discussed in our telephone conversation this morning, the Colloquium will take place on June 29 in the convention room at the Blackduck Inn.

The Colloquium will begin with the keynote address at 10:30 A.M. At 11:00, you will join our other guests of honor in a debate on the topic, "The Cost of Conservation: Public or Private Responsibilities?" Following the debate, luncheon will be served in the main dining room, where you will, of course, be a guest of the Committee.

Along with the other members of the Committee, I am looking forward to our meeting on the 29th.

Sincerely yours,

Charles Mapes
Event Coordinator

Figure 4–2
Follow-Up

Confirmations

While confirmations are routine for such businesses as hotels and travel agencies, other businesses may also require them. Doctors, for example, and repair services can avoid wasted time by contacting patients and customers a day or so in advance of scheduled appointments. Such confirmations are frequently made by telephone or e-mail, but a form letter or postcard also effectively transmits *clear, correct,* and *complete* information, particularly when the type of business requires large numbers of confirmations. As is often the case, however, an individually written letter, such as Figure 4–3, can turn a customer into a *regular* customer by adding a personal touch.

The Barclay

123 South 96th Street, Omaha, Nebraska 68114
(800) 555-1234   *www.anycompany.com*

August 10, 20–

Mr. Yegor Volsky
2 Connecticut Avenue, N.W.
Washington, D.C. 20006

Dear Mr. Volsky:

This letter will confirm your reservation for a single room with bath for August 24–27. Your room will be available after 2 P.M. on the 24th.

Since you will be arriving in Omaha by plane, you may want to take advantage of The Barclay's Shuttle. Our limousine departs from the domestic terminal every hour on the half hour, and the service is free for guests of the hotel.

Cordially yours,

Hassan Khalid
Assistant Manager

Figure 4–3
Confirmation

Remittances

Companies often request that their bill, or a portion of their bill, accompany a remittance. When this is not the case, a cover letter is necessary to explain what your enclosed check is for. This letter should contain any information regarding your order that will be needed for the proper crediting of your account: include your account number, the invoice number, and the amount of the check. **Do not** include superfluous information that could confuse an accounts-receivable clerk. Remarks not directly related to the remittance should be reserved for a separate letter.

EXAMPLE

Dear Sirs:

The enclosed check for $312.68 is in payment of invoice no. 10463. Please credit my account (no. 663-711-M).

Yours truly,

Order Acknowledgments

Many companies today have abandoned the practice of acknowledging orders, particularly when the order will be filled promptly. Some companies respond to orders by immediately sending an invoice, and some employ the halfway measure of using printed acknowledgment forms. But however handled, confirming an order helps to establish goodwill by reassuring the customer that the order has been received.

First orders **should** be acknowledged in order to welcome the new customer and encourage further business (Figure 4–4). Similarly, an unusually large order by a regular customer deserves a note of appreciation.

Any order acknowledgment, whatever the circumstances, should contain specific information. It should let the customer know exactly what is being done about the order by:

1. mentioning the date of the order;
2. including the order or invoice number;
3. explaining the date and method of shipment;
4. acknowledging the method of payment.

Of course, all order acknowledgments should also express your appreciation for the order and assure the customer that it will be filled.

An acknowledgment is often an opportunity for a sales pitch. First of all, if a salesperson was involved in the order, his or her name should appear somewhere in the letter. But beyond this, a letter may also include a description of the merchandise to reaffirm the wisdom of the customer's purchase. Other related products may also be mentioned to spark the customer's interest and future orders.

pp

PAYTON'S PLASTICS, INC.
13 Spruce Street
Philadelphia, PA 19102
(800) 555-1234
www.anycompany.com

September 16, 20–

Ms. Cybel Megan
FRAMES-BY-YOU
126 Walnut Street
Philadelphia, PA 19102

Dear Ms. Megan:

We are pleased to have received your order of September 15 and would like to welcome you as a new customer of Payton's Plastics.

Your order (No. 62997) for one dozen 4′ × 5′ sheets of 1/8″ Lucite is being processed and will be ready for shipment on September 21. It will be delivered to your workshop by our own van, and payment will be c.o.d. (our policy for all orders under $100).

We are sure you will appreciate the clear finish and tensile strength of our entire line of plastics. Ms. Julie Methel, your sales representative, will call on you soon with a catalog and samples.

Cordially,

PAYTON'S PLASTICS, INC.

Howard Roberts
Customer Relations

Figure 4–4
Order Acknowledgment

Because orders cannot always be filled promptly and smoothly, situations arise in which a wise businessperson will send more than a mere acknowledgment.

Customers, for example, cannot always be relied on to submit complete orders. When an essential piece of information has been omitted, the order must be delayed and a tactful letter sent. Although the customer in such a case is at fault, the letter must neither place any blame nor express impatience. Indeed, the customer's own impatience must be allayed with a positive, friendly tone. A bit of reselling—reminding the customer of the order's desirability—is often useful in a letter of this kind.

EXAMPLE

Dear Mr. Yuan:

Thank you for your order of October 22 for six rolls of black nylon webbing. We are eager to deliver Order 129 to your store as soon as possible.

But first, please let us know whether you'd like the webbing in 1-, $1\frac{1}{3}$-, or $2\frac{1}{2}$-inch widths. If you note your preference on the bottom of this letter and mail or fax it back to us today, we can have your order ready by the beginning of next week.

Olsen's Upholstery products are among the finest made, and we're sure you'd like to receive your purchase without further delay.

Sincerely yours,

Sometimes a *delayed delivery* is caused by the seller, not the buyer—a delicate situation that requires a carefully written letter (Figure 4–5). When an order cannot be filled promptly, the customer is entitled to an explanation. Assurance should be given that the delay is unavoidable and that everything is being done to speed delivery.

Such a letter must be especially *you* oriented. It should express that you understand the customer's disappointment and regret the inconvenience. At the same time, the letter must avoid a negative tone and not only stress that the merchandise is worth waiting for but also assume that the customer is willing to wait. The form letter in Figure 4–5 could be used in a mass mailing but sounds, nevertheless, as if it has the individual customer in mind.

5555 Third Avenue

American Electric Company, Inc.

New York, New York 10021
(800) 555-1234
www.anycompany.com

Dear

Requests for our pamphlet, "10 Points to Consider When Buying Home Video Equipment," have been overwhelming. As a result, we are temporarily out of copies.

Nevertheless, the new printing is presently being prepared, and I have added your name to the mailing list to receive a copy as soon as it is available.

In the meantime, you may find an article by Professor Leonard Mack, of the Pennsylvania Institute of Technology, to be of some help. The article, entitled "The Latest Crop of Home Video Centers," appeared in the September issue of *Consumer Digest*.

Sincerely,

Hassam El Tawdy
Customer Service

Figure 4–5
Delayed Delivery

When a *partial shipment* can be made, the customer must be informed that certain items have been *back-ordered*. Again, the letter should assume the customer's willingness to wait. It should also make an attempt to "resell" the merchandise by stressing its finer features without emphasizing the missing items (see Figure 4–6).

Silver Imports, Ltd.
6023 San Anselmo Avenue
San Anselmo, California 94960
(800) 555-1234
www.anycompany.com

March 4, 20–

Ms. Bonnie Corum
Bonnie's Baubles
4091 West Ninth Street
Winston-Salem, North Carolina 27102

Dear Ms. Corum:

Thank you for your recent order, number 622. We are always especially delighted to serve an old friend.

Your six pairs of Chinese Knot earrings (item 15b) and one dozen Primrose pendants (item 8a) have been shipped by United Parcel and should arrive at your boutique within the week.

Unfortunately, our stock of cloisonné bangle bracelets (item 9d) has been depleted because of a delay in shipments from China. Our craftsmen have been at great pains to keep up with the demand for these intricate and finely wrought bracelets. We have put your one dozen bracelets on back order and hope to have them on their way to you before the end of the month.

Very truly yours,

Chun Lee Ng
Manager

Figure 4–6
Partial Delivery

When an order cannot be filled at all, a letter suggesting a *substitute order* (Figure 4–7) is occasionally appropriate. The suggested merchandise must, naturally, be comparable to the original order and should be offered from a perspective not of salvaging a sale, but of helping the customer. The letter must include a sales pitch for the suggested item, but it should emphasize the customer's needs. Of course, the letter should also explain why the original order cannot be filled.

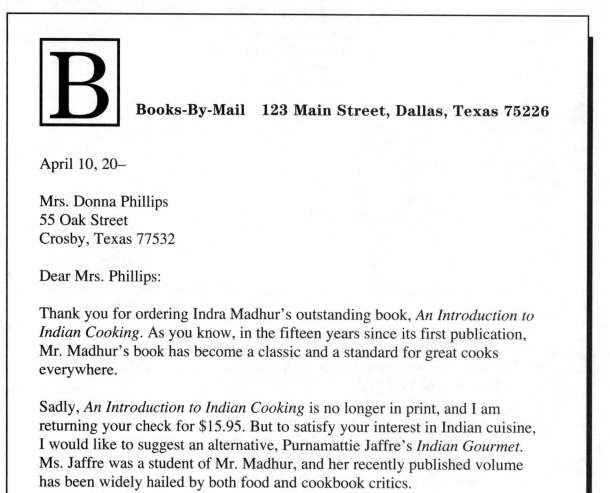

B Books-By-Mail   123 Main Street, Dallas, Texas 75226

April 10, 20–

Mrs. Donna Phillips
55 Oak Street
Crosby, Texas 77532

Dear Mrs. Phillips:

Thank you for ordering Indra Madhur's outstanding book, *An Introduction to Indian Cooking*. As you know, in the fifteen years since its first publication, Mr. Madhur's book has become a classic and a standard for great cooks everywhere.

Sadly, *An Introduction to Indian Cooking* is no longer in print, and I am returning your check for $15.95. But to satisfy your interest in Indian cuisine, I would like to suggest an alternative, Purnamattie Jaffre's *Indian Gourmet*. Ms. Jaffre was a student of Mr. Madhur, and her recently published volume has been widely hailed by both food and cookbook critics.

If you would like a copy of *Indian Gourmet*, which costs only $13.95, please let me know, and I will immediately send it to you.

Cordially,

David Ewing
Order Department

Figure 4–7
Substitute Delivery

Stopgap Letters

When a thorough response to an incoming letter must be delayed, receipt of the letter should nevertheless be promptly acknowledged. Such letters of acknowledgment are called **stopgap letters**. They let your customer know that his inquiry has not been ignored and will be attended to as soon as possible.

Like a delayed delivery letter, a stopgap letter informs your customer that time is needed to process the request. Necessary information or materials, for example, may not be immediately available. Or your company may have prescribed channels for reacting to certain inquiries. Credit applications and insurance claims, for instance, take time to be processed and so are often answered promptly with a stopgap acknowledgment.

A stopgap letter will also be called for when your employer is out of town. The correspondent should be assured that the letter will be relayed to your employer as soon as he or she returns. You should be careful **not** to commit your employer to any action, nor should you explain his absence.

EXAMPLE

Dear Reverend Hollingsworth:

Your request to meet with Rabbi Tucker to discuss his participating in an interfaith symposium on world peace arrived this morning. However, Rabbi Tucker is out of town and is not expected back before the 15th.

I will be sure to inform the rabbi of the planned symposium as soon as he returns.

Yours truly,

Inquiry Replies

All inquiries should be answered, even those that cannot for some reason be given a complete response. An inquiry indicates interest in your company and a potential customer. The inquiry reply should be designed not only to increase that interest but to inspire the inquirer to action.

An inquiry reply should begin by thanking the reader, acknowledging the interest in your company. As in Figure 4–8, it should end by offering further assistance—but **only** if you actually want additional inquiries from this person.

The substance of an inquiry reply is usually *information*. You should include not only the specific facts your correspondent requested but any others that may be of help. (This is, of course, assuming that the original inquiry or request was reasonable.) If you cannot provide all the relevant data right away, you should promise it.

If the information requested cannot be provided at all (as in Figure 4–9), if it is confidential, you should explain this in your letter. You must be careful, however, to word your explanation tactfully and resist the impulse to accuse your reader of trying to gather information to which she is not entitled. Assume the inquiry was innocent and try to maintain goodwill.

A&M Sewing Supplies, Inc. 40-04 Summit Avenue, Fairlawn, NJ 07410

June 2, 20–

Mr. Samuel Long
Maxine Sportswear Manufacturing Co., Inc.
607 Grand Street
New York, New York 10002

Dear Mr. Long:

Thank you for your interest in A & M equipment. We are happy to supply you with the information you requested.

The following prices are quoted per dozen. Individual units are slightly higher:

Item	1 Dozen @:
A-1 Garment Turner	$180.00
A-1 Automatic Winder	90.00
Ace Thread Trimmer	120.00
No-Slip Feed Puller	132.00

In case you have any further questions, Mr. Long, please do not hesitate to call. I can be reached between 8:30 A.M. and 6:00 P.M. at (800) 555–1234.

Sincerely yours,

Brevia Short
Sales Representative

Figure 4–8
Inquiry Reply I

Maxine Sportswear Manufacturing Co., Inc.

607 Grand Avenue, New York, NY 10002

June 10, 20–

Mrs. Athina Stratakis
63 Pelham Parkway
Bronx, New York 10467

Dear Mrs. Stratakis

We certainly appreciate your interest in Maxine Sportswear. Nevertheless,
I am afraid I cannot supply you with the information you request.

Because we do not sell our garments directly to the consumer, we try to keep
our wholesale prices between ourselves and our dealers. It is our way of
meriting both the loyalty and good faith of those with whom we do business.
Clearly, divulging our wholesale prices to a consumer would be a violation
of a trust.

However, I have enclosed for your reference a list of our dealers in the
Bronx and Manhattan. A number of these dealers sell Maxine Sportswear
at discount.

Very truly yours

Samuel Long
Assistant Vice President

Figure 4–9
Inquiry Reply II

Sometimes a request for information about a company's products or services may be answered with a brochure or catalog. Such materials, though, must always be accompanied by a personalized cover letter. You should explain why you've sent the brochure and arouse your reader's interest in it; you should also call attention to the particulars of the brochure and attempt to encourage a sale.

A good practice for a manufacturer who doesn't sell directly to the public is to pass along copies of the inquiry and reply to a dealer, who may pursue the sale further.

Dear Mr. Erlander:

Thank you for your request for information about the Teaneck Tennis Center. As one of New Jersey's newest facilities, we are a full-service tennis club just 15 minutes from Manhattan.

The enclosed brochure describes our special features, including championship-size courts and professional instruction. You may find the section on our Businessperson's Special of particular interest.

If you drop by Teaneck Tennis any time between 7 A.M. and 10 P.M., we would be delighted to give you a personal tour of the Center—at no obligation of course.

Cordially yours,

Referrals

Businesspeople often receive inquiries that can best be answered by another person. In that case, the correspondent must be informed that the inquiry is being passed on.

A letter of referral should *acknowledge receipt* of the inquiry and *explain* why and to whom it is being referred. Alternately, you may find it more efficient to advise the correspondent of the proper source of information and tell exactly where to write.

Again, a manufacturer should be especially careful to sustain the readers' interest even while referring them to a dealer. The address of a local dealer or a list of dealers in the area should be included in this kind of referral. Too, customers should *never* be chastised for bypassing intermediaries; instead, they should be politely referred to the appropriate source.

Dear Mrs. Simpson:

Your request for information regarding marriage counselors in your community can best be answered by the Board of Community Services.

I am therefore referring your letter to Mr. Orlando Ortiz at the Whitestone Community Board. He will, I am sure, be in touch with you soon.

Yours truly,

Refusals

There are many times when a businessperson must say no. When granting a favor, awarding a contract, hiring an applicant, or for that matter making any decision, saying yes to one person often means saying no to another. The key, however, is to say no gracefully. Here, as in most correspondence, maintaining goodwill is extremely important.

When saying no, you should first of all never actually say *no*. Your letter should be as positive as you can make it. The actual refusal should be stated once and briefly. The rest of the letter should be reader oriented and very friendly.

No matter what the request, your reader deserves an explanation of your refusal. Your reason should be based on facts, not emotions, although an appeal to your reader's sense of fairplay or business savvy is

---

AGNES CAFIERO, M.D.

California Institute of Psychiatry
1052 Seventh Avenue
San Francisco, California 94118
888-555-1234

September 1, 20–

The Honorable Nelson McKenzie
The State Capitol Building
Sacramento, California 95814

Dear Mr. McKenzie:

Thank you for your recent request for my endorsement of your campaign for United States Senator. I am honored that you believe my name could be of value to you.

My professional policy, however, is to refrain from public endorsements. In my practice, I treat patients of all political parties, and I strongly believe that it is in their best interest that I maintain a nonpartisan position.

Privately, of course, I allow myself more leeway. I have always been impressed by your stand on the issues, particularly your support for national health insurance. I wish you all the best in your campaign and am enclosing a personal contribution of $100.

Sincerely yours,

Agnes Cafiero, M.D.

Figure 4–10
Refusal

often appropriate (see Figure 4–10). NEVER make the reader the reason for your refusal.

Rarely in a refusal will you want to sever all business connections. Therefore, you should be careful to keep your letter "open-ended." Express appreciation for the request even though it is being denied, and if possible suggest an alternative course of action. A "not-at-this-time" refusal keeps open the possibility of future business.

▉▉▉▉▉▉▉ PRACTICE CORRESPONDENCE

Prepare a letter of response for each of the following situations.

A. You are employed in the shipping department of Kinbote Products, Inc., 123 West Flagler Street, Miami, Florida 33131. Write a letter acknowledging the following order from Ellen Minsky, buyer for Gold's Specialty Shops, 2 Busch Boulevard, Tampa, Florida 33607.

Dear Sirs:

Please send me two dozen exercise suits (Style L-29) in the following assortment of sizes and colors:

Vanilla–3 petite, 3 small, 4 medium, 2 large
Chocolate–2 petite, 4 small, 4 medium, 2 large

Charge my account (882GSS) for the wholesale price of $35 per suit.

I would like the order shipped air express and would appreciate your letting me know how soon I may expect delivery.

Yours truly,

B. Cornell Peal, vice-president of the General Communications Corporation, 123 Corporate Drive, Milwaukee, Wisconsin 53202, is out of town attending a four-day meeting of the regional directors of the company. As his administrative assistant, send a stopgap letter in response to the following request from Professor Anne Boleyn, Department of Media and Communications, University of Wisconsin, Menomonie, Wisconsin 54751.

Dear Mr. Peal:

Last month, I telephoned your office to invite you to give a guest lecture to my graduate seminar in teletronics. You said you would be pleased to give such a lecture but asked that I contact you again, in writing, later in the semester.

If you are still interested in visiting the class, I would very much like to set a date for the lecture. The class meets on Tuesdays from 4:30 to 6:00 P.M. and runs for six more weeks.

I would appreciate your letting me know as soon as possible which Tuesday would be most convenient for you.

Sincerely yours,

C. You have just made a luncheon engagement for your employer Sook Chang, an architect with Fulson Contractors, Inc., 4444 West Rockies Avenue, Boulder, Colorado 80301. The appointment is with a prospective client, Justin Michaels, 123 Auburn Street, Aurora, Colorado 80321. Write a letter to Mr. Michaels to confirm the lunch date, which will take place at Trattoria di Marco, at the corner of Tenth Street and Western Avenue, on April 7 at 1 P.M.

D. You are employed by the Lawsen Linen Company, P.O. Box 999, Bloomfield, New Jersey 07003. Write a letter to Mrs. Marianne Rollins, 444 Maple Avenue, Caldwell, New Jersey 07006, to explain a delay in shipping her order for one set of Floral Mist queen-size sheets and pillowcases. Because of a factory strike, all orders have been held up, but assure her that negotiations are progressing and a settlement is expected soon. Convince her to wait and not cancel her order.

E. Arthur Edwards, owner of Edwards Drug Store, 123 Peachtree Street, Atlanta, Georgia 30309, has been a customer of the Southern Cosmetics Company, 755 Lakeland Turnpike, Macon, Georgia 30326, for seven years. Because Mr. Edwards has placed an unusually large order, he has requested a special discount. As a representative of Southern Cosmetics, write a letter to Mr. Edwards refusing the discount.

5.
Credit and Collection Letters

Credit Letters

Credit involves the purchasing and receiving of goods without immediate payment. Being able to "buy now and pay later" enables a purchaser to acquire desired goods even when cash is not currently available. Allowing individuals and businesses to buy on credit can increase a company's volume of sales. Therefore, buying and selling on credit have become a common and essential business practice.

Of course, before granting credit, a company must be reasonably sure of the customer's financial stability and ability and willingness to pay. These are verified by the exchange of credit information. Five types of letters are involved in credit correspondence:

1. applications for credit
2. inquiries about credit worthiness
3. responses about credit worthiness
4. letters granting credit
5. letters refusing credit

Applications

Consumer applications for charge accounts, with businesses such as department stores or gasoline companies, are usually made by filling out an application blank. This form typically allows space for home and business addresses, names of banks and account numbers, a list of other charge accounts, and, perhaps, a list of references.

Business account applications are more often made by letter (Figure 5–1). A new business, for example, may wish to place a first order with a supplier or manufacturer and establish a credit line or open account. A letter of this kind should include credit references (such as banks and other businesses that have extended credit).

Credit Inquiries

Large retailers usually turn credit applications over to a *credit bureau*. Such bureaus keep files on people and businesses whose credit references and histories they have investigated. When they determine an applicant's *credit standing* (that is, reputation for financial stability), they give the applicant a *credit rating* (the bureau's evaluation of the credit standing). On the basis of this rating, the retailer decides whether or not to grant the applicant credit.

When checking a business's credit standing, a company may contact the references. The letter of credit inquiry (see Figure 5–2) should contain all known information about the applicant, and it should assure the reference that all information will remain confidential. The inclusion of a reply envelope is a wise courtesy.

KRETCHMER'S APPLIANCE STORE
1135 STATE STREET, CHICAGO, ILLINOIS 60604
TEL. 800-555-1234   FAX (555) 123-4567

February 3, 20–

Standard Electric Corporation
2120 Oak Terrace
Lake Bluff, Illinois 60044

Dear Madam or Sir:

Enclosed is our purchase order 121 for 6 four-slice toasters, model 18E.

We would like to place this order on open account according to your regular terms. Our store has been open for two months, and you may check our credit rating with Ms. Keisha Sawyer, branch manager of the First Bank of Chicago, 1160 State Street, Chicago, Illinois 60604.

You may also check our credit standing with the following companies:

The Kenso Clock Company, 2390 Ottawa Avenue, Grand Rapids, Michigan 49503

National Kitchen Products, Inc., 400 East Main Street, Round Lake Park, Illinois 60073

Eastern Electric Corporation, 750 East 58th Street, Chicago, Illinois 60637

Please let us know your decision regarding our credit as well as an approximate delivery date for our first order.

Sincerely yours,

Bruce Kretchmer

Figure 5–1
Credit Application

Credit Responses

Companies that receive large numbers of credit inquiries often use their own form for responding. In this way, they can control the information given out and, especially, limit the information to hard facts: amounts owed and presently due, maximum credit allowed, the dates of account's opening and last sale, degree of promptness in payment, etc.

Standard Electric Corporation

2120 Oak Terrace
Lake Bluff, Illinois 60044
800-555-1234
www.anycompany.com

February 7, 20–

Ms. Keisha Sawyer
Branch Manager
The First Bank of Chicago
1160 State Street
Chicago, Illinois 60604

Dear Ms. Sawyer:

Kretchmer's Appliance Store, 1135 State Street, Chicago, has placed an order with us for $120 worth of merchandise and listed you as a credit reference.

We would appreciate your sending us information regarding Kretchmer's credit rating. We would especially like to know how long the owner, Bruce Kretchmer, has had an account with you and whether or not any of his debts are past due. We will, of course, keep any information we receive in the strictest confidence.

A reply envelope is enclosed for your convenience.

Sincerely yours,

STANDARD ELECTRIC CORPORATION

Milton Smedley
Credit Department

Figure 5–2
Credit Inquiry

Because an individual's or business's reputation is at stake, opinions should be expressed discreetly, if at all. Particularly when a credit reference is unfavorable, it is advisable to state only objective facts in order to avoid a possible libel suit. Most companies, moreover, reiterate somewhere in the letter (see Figure 5–3) that they expect the information provided to remain confidential.

The First Bank Of Chicago
1160 State Street
Chicago, Illinois 60604
(800) 555-1234

February 14, 20–

Mr. Milton Smedley
Credit Department
Standard Electric Corporation
2120 Oak Terrace
Lake Bluff, Illinois 60044

Dear Mr. Smedley:

We are happy to send you, in confidence, the credit information you requested concerning Mr. Bruce Kretchmer, owner of Kretchmer's Appliance Store.

Mr. Kretchmer, who was appliance department supervisor at Lillian's Department Store until last fall, has had personal checking and savings accounts with us for the past ten years. His accounts were always in order, with adequate balances to cover all checks drawn.

His appliance store, at 1135 State Street, was opened last December. For this undertaking, he borrowed $20,000 from this bank and has begun making regular payments against the loan. We are unaware of any further outstanding debts he may have.

On the basis of our experience with him, we believe Mr. Kretchmer to be credit worthy.

Yours truly,

THE FIRST BANK OF CHICAGO

Keisha Sawyer
Branch Manager

Figure 5–3
Credit Reference

Credit-Granting Letters

When all credit references are favorable, a letter is sent granting credit to the customer (Figure 5–4). Whether for a consumer charge account or a dealer open account, the acceptance letter should:

Standard Electric Corporation

2120 Oak Terrace
Lake Bluff, Illinois 60044
(800) 555-1234
www.anycompany.com

February 18, 20–

Mr. Bruce Kretchmer
Kretchmer's Appliance Store
1135 State Street
Chicago, Illinois 60604

Dear Mr. Kretchmer:

It is my pleasure to welcome you as an SEC credit customer as your request for credit has been approved.

Your first order, for 6 Model 18E toasters, will be ready for shipment on Monday, February 22.

On the first of each month, we will prepare a statement of the previous month's purchases. Your payment is due in full on the tenth. With each statement, you will also receive notice of special dealer options, such as advertising campaigns, rebate programs, and closeouts.

Arlene Ryan, your personal SEC sales representative, will visit you sometime next week. In addition to bringing you catalogs and samples, she will explain how to place orders online or by phone with our voice recognition system.

We are delighted that SEC can be a part of your store's beginnings and look forward to serving you for many years to come.

Sincerely yours,

Milton Smedley
Credit Department

Figure 5–4
Credit-Granting Letter

1. approve the credit;
2. welcome the customer and express appreciation;
3. explain the credit terms and privileges;
4. establish goodwill and encourage further sales.

Credit-Refusing Letters

Sometimes, of course, credit must be denied (Figure 5–5). A letter refusing credit must give the customer a reason, which, however, may be expressed vaguely for purposes of tact and protection of references.

The credit-refusing letter must also try to encourage business on a cash basis; the tone, therefore, must be positive and in some way *"you* oriented."

HANS & MEYER'S ▪ Suppliers to the Plumbing Trade ▪ 9090 Broadway, New York, NY 10003

August 10, 20–

Mr. Donald Cortland
Cortland Hardware Store
20-67 Kissena Blvd.
Queens, NY 11367

Dear Mr. Cortland:

Thank you for your recent application for Hans & Meyer's 60-day terms of credit. However, we believe it would not be in your best interest to grant you credit at this time.

An impartial credit investigation indicates that your company's present financial obligations are substantial. We fear that adding to those obligations could jeopardize your sound credit standing in the community.

Of course, Mr. Cortland, you are always welcome to buy from Hans & Meyer's on a COD basis. We will try our best to serve you in all ways possible. And if, in the future, your obligations should be reduced, feel free to apply again for terms of credit. We shall be delighted to reconsider.

Cordially yours,

Leonard Meyer
Vice President

Figure 5–5
Credit-Refusing Letter

In addition, it is a good idea to suggest that these customers reapply for credit in the future, thereby letting them know that you desire and appreciate their business.

Collection Letters

No matter how carefully a company screens its credit customers, there will be times when a bill goes unpaid and steps to collect must be taken. The problem when writing a collection letter is how to exact payment and simultaneously keep a customer. The writer of a collection letter wants to get the money owed *and* maintain goodwill.

Collection letters, therefore, should be *persuasive* rather than forceful, *firm* rather than demanding. A fair and tactful letter gets better results than a sarcastic or abusive one. In fact, even collection letters should be "*you* oriented": courteous, considerate, and concerned about the customer's best interest.

Collection letters are usually sent in a series. The first letter is mildest and most understanding, with the letters becoming gradually more insistent. The final letter in a series, when all previous letters have failed, threatens to turn the matter over to a lawyer or collection agency. Of course, the tone of any letter in the series will vary, from positive and mild to negative and strong, depending upon the past payment record of the customer. The time between the letters may also vary, from ten days to a month at the start, from one to two weeks later on.

Every letter in a collection series contains certain information:

1. the amount owed;
2. how long the bill is overdue;
3. a specific action the customer may take.

Some companies also like to include a **sales appeal**, even late in the series, as an extra incentive for payment.

In general, most bills are paid within ten days of receipt, with nearly all the rest being paid within the month. Therefore, when a bill is a month overdue, action is called for. Still, the collection process must begin gently—frequently with a telephone call. Should this fail to get results, the letter series begins.

Step 1

The *monthly statement* reminds the customer of outstanding bills. If it is ignored, it should be followed (about a week or ten days later) by a second statement. The second statement should contain a notice (in the form of a rubber stamp or sticker) stating "Past Due" or "Please Remit." An alternative is to include a card or slip with the statement, alerting the customer to the overdue bill. This notice should be phrased in formal, possibly even stilted language; it is an *objective* reminder that does not prematurely embarrass the customer with too early a personal appeal.

> Our records indicate that the balance of $_____ on your account is now past due. Payment is requested.

Step 2

If the objective statement and reminder fail to get results, the collection process must gradually become more emotional and personal. (Form letters may be used, but they should *look* personal, adapted to the specific situation.) The second collection message, however, should still be friendly. It should seek to excuse the unpaid bill as an oversight; the tone should convey the assumption that the customer intends to pay. At this stage, too, a stress on future sales, rather than on payment, may induce action.

COLLECTION LETTER I

Dear _____ :

Snow may still be on the ground, but the first signs of spring are already budding. And we know you will be planning your Spring Sales soon.

When you send us a check for $ _____ , now _____ past due, you will guarantee that your next order will be promptly filled.

Oversights, of course, do happen, but we know you won't want to miss the opportunity, not only of stocking up for the coming season, but of taking advantage of our seasonal ad campaign as well.

Sincerely yours,

Step 3

The next letter in the series should still be friendly, but it should also now be firm. While expressing confidence in the customer's intention to pay, it should inquire about the *reason* for the delay. The third collection message should also make an appeal to the customer's sense of:

1. fairness;
2. cooperation;
3. obligation;

or desire to:

1. save her credit reputation;
2. maintain her credit line.

This letter should stress the customer's self-interest by pointing out the importance of prompt payment and the dangers of losing credit standing. The letter should convey the urgency and seriousness of the situation.

COLLECTION LETTER II

Dear _____ :

We are truly at a loss. We cannot understand why you still have not cleared your balance of $ _____ , which is now _____ overdue.

Although you have been a reliable customer for _____ years, we are afraid you are placing your credit standing in jeopardy. Only you, by sending us a check today, can secure the continued convenience of buying on credit.

We would hate to lose a valued friend, Mr./Ms. _____ .

Please allow us to keep serving you.

Sincerely,

Step 4

Ultimately, payment must be demanded. The threat of legal action or the intervention of a collection agency is sometimes all that will induce a customer to pay. In some companies, moreover, an executive other than the credit manager signs this last letter as a means of impressing the customer with the finality of the situation. Still, the fourth collection letter allows the customer one last chance to pay before steps are taken.

> **Note:** Before threatening legal action, it is advisable to have a **final collection letter** reviewed by an attorney.

FINAL COLLECTION LETTER

Dear _____ :

Our Collection Department has informed me of its intention to file suit as you have failed to answer any of our requests for payment of $ _____ , which is now _____ overdue.

Before taking this action, however, I would like to make a personal appeal to your sound business judgment. I feel certain that if you telephone me, we can devise some means to settle this matter out of court.

Therefore, I ask that you get in touch with me by the _____ of the month so that I may avoid taking steps that neither of us would like.

Truly yours,

> **Note:** If a customer responds to a collection letter, **stop the collection series**, even if the response is not full payment.

A customer may, for example, offer an excuse or promise payment; he may make a partial payment or request special payment arrangements. In such cases, the series would be inappropriate.

For instance, if your customer has owed $6000 on account for two months and sends you a check for $1500, you may send a letter such as the following:

PARTIAL PAYMENT ACKNOWLEDGMENT

Dear Mr. Marsh:

Thank you for your check for $1500. The balance remaining on your account is now $4500.

Since you have requested an extension, we offer you the following payment plan: $1500 by the 15th of the month for the next three months.

If you have another plan in mind, please telephone my office so that we may discuss it. Otherwise, we will expect your next check for $1500 on September 15.

Sincerely yours,

■■■■■ PRACTICE CORRESPONDENCE

For each of the following, prepare a credit or collection letter, as specified in the directions.

A. Mr. Marvin Gold of 1602 Arlington Avenue, Bronx, New York 10477, has had a charge account at Manson's Department Store, 4404 Madison Avenue, New York, New York 10010, for six years. His credit limit is $7000. He has always paid his bills on time although he currently has an outstanding balance of $182.54, forty-five days overdue. The National Credit Bureau has contacted Manson's for credit information about Mr. Gold. Write the letter Manson's should send to the National Credit Bureau.

B. The credit references of Ms. Migdalia Ruiz (818 Ocean Parkway, Brooklyn, New York 11230) are all favorable, and so her new charge account with Manson's Department Store has been approved. Write the letter Manson's should send to Ms. Ruiz.

C. Ms. Hiroko Osawa's credit references indicate that, although she has no outstanding debts or record of poor payment, her employment history is unstable. Manson's Department Store, therefore, concludes that she would be a poor credit risk. Write the letter that Manson's should send to Ms. Osawa (6061 Valentine Lane, Yonkers, New York 10705), denying her application for a charge account.

D. Weimar's Furniture Emporium (617 Sherman Road, North Hollywood, California 91605) has owed the Eastgate Furniture Manufacturing Company, Inc., $750 for forty-five days. Eastgate has sent two statements and one letter, which Weimar's has ignored. Write the next letter that Eastgate (4000 Bush Street, San Francisco, California 94108) should send to Weimar's.

E. For eight years, Mr. Josef Larsen, of 1 Penny Lane, Summit, Pennsylvania 17214, has been a charge customer of Browne's Department Store (9 Chestnut Street, Philadelphia, Pennsylvania 19107). A "slow pay," he has nevertheless always remitted within sixty days of purchase. However, Mr. Larsen's balance of $269.48 is now ninety days past due. He has not responded to the two statements and two letters Browne's has already sent him. Write the next letter that Browne's should send to Mr. Larsen.

6.
Complaints, Claims, and Adjustments

Business transactions will from time to time go awry, and the exchange of money, merchandise, or service will not occur as expected. In such situations, the customer must promptly notify the company of the problem by letter; such a letter is logically called a *complaint*. A complaint that calls upon the company to make restitution is called a *claim*. The company, responding to the claim, will write a letter of *adjustment*.

Complaints

When a customer is dissatisfied with goods or services, a complaint letter (Figure 6–1) will inform the company or organization of the problem. Such a letter should both present the facts and express the customer's dissatisfaction.

Because a complaint, unlike a claim, does not necessarily call for action or compensation from the company, it should be answered gracefully (Figure 6–2). Indeed, the writer of a complaint is offering help to the offending organization, an opportunity to improve its operations. Therefore, the response to a complaint should be concerned and courteous, *not* defensive. It may offer an explanation and suggest remedies that are being followed. It definitely should extend an apology.

Claims

Countless aspects of business dealings can break down, but the most common causes for claims are:

1. an incorrect bill, invoice, or statement (Figure 6–3);
2. a bill for merchandise ordered but never received;
3. delivery of unordered merchandise;
4. delivery of incorrect merchandise;
5. delivery of damaged or defective merchandise (Figure 6–4);
6. an unusually delayed delivery.

Two other more specialized types of claims are:

1. a request for an adjustment under a guarantee or warranty;
2. a request for restitution under an insurance policy.

21 West Main Street
Cochecton, NY 12725
October 9, 20—

Dr. Linda Peters, Director
County General Hospital
Route 97
Callicoon, New York 12723

Dear Dr. Peters:

On the afternoon of October 8, my neighbor's son, Kevin DiMaria,
was raking leaves in his family's yard when he tripped and fell.
From the degree of pain he was obviously experiencing, I sus-
pected he might have broken his ankle. Thus, as the only adult
around at the time, I drove him to your hospital.

When we arrived at the emergency room, no one was available to
help Kevin from the car, and I had to help him hobble in as best I
could. The effort increased his pain, yet when we were inside, the
receptionist, without looking up, told us to take a number and wait
our turn. We waited for more than two hours before Kevin was
seen by a doctor.

As a member of the community your hospital serves, I am outraged
by the treatment my young neighbor received. The lack of
concern was upsetting; the lack of attention could have been life
threatening. All of us in Wayne County deserve better treatment,
and I hope you will look into the situation to see that the suffering
endured by Kevin DiMaria is never again inflicted by an employee
of your institution.

Yours truly,

Michelle Sussman

Figure 6–1
Complaint

County General Hospital
Route 97
Callicoon, NY 12723
888-555-1234

October 12, 20—

Ms. Michelle Sussman
21 West Main Street
Cochecton, New York 12725

Dear Ms. Sussman:

Thank you for bringing to my attention the inexcusable wait you and Kevin DiMaria endured in the emergency room on October 8. I am extremely sorry for any additional pain Kevin may have experienced and any emotional stress you may have felt under the circumstances.

Allow me, however, to offer an explanation. Shortly before you arrived, an automobile accident just outside Callicoon resulted in four seriously injured people being rushed to County General. Since we are, as you know, a small rural hospital, our emergency staff was stretched to its limits to assist these people simultaneously.

Nevertheless, you and Kevin should not have been ignored for two hours. I have spoken to the receptionist with whom you dealt, and I can assure you that, in the future, arrivals to our emergency room will be treated with concern and prompt attention.

Again, I apologize for the events of October 8 and greatly appreciate your letting me know about them.

Yours truly,

Linda Peters, M.D.

Figure 6–2
Complaint Response

A claim is written to *inform* the company of the problem and *suggest* a fair compensation. No matter how infuriating the nature of the problem nor how great the inconvenience, the purpose of a claim is **not** to express anger but to get results.

Therefore, it is important to avoid a hostile or demanding tone. A claim must be calm and polite but also firm.

A claim should begin with the facts, first explaining the problem (such as the condition of the merchandise or the specific error made). Then all the necessary details should be recounted in a logical order. These details may include the order and delivery dates, the order or invoice number, the account number, the method of shipment, etc. A copy of proof of purchase, such as a sales slip or an invoice, should be included whenever possible. (Always, of course, retain the original.)

Remember: You are more likely to receive a favorable response from an adjuster who understands your problem thoroughly.

---

811 Regent Street
Phoenix, Arizona 85027
December 3, 20—

Gleason's Department Store
2297 Front Street
Phoenix, Arizona 85007

Attention: Billing Department

Dear Sir or Madam:

I have just received the November statement on my charge account (No. 059-3676). The statement lists a purchase for $83.95, including tax, which I am sure I did not make.

This purchase was supposedly made in Department 08 on November 12. But because I was out of town the week of the tenth and no one else is authorized to use my account, I am sure the charge is in error.

I have checked all the other items on the statement against my sales receipts, and they all seem to be correct. I am therefore deducting the $83.95 from the balance on the statement and sending you a check for $155.75.

I would appreciate your looking into this matter so that my account may be cleared.

Sincerely yours,

Rosetta Falco

Figure 6–3
Claim I

The second part of the claim should emphasize the loss or inconvenience that has been suffered. Again, the account should be factual and unemotional, and naturally you should **not** exaggerate.

Finally, you should state a *reasonable* adjustment. This should be worded positively and convey your confidence that the company will be fair.

As you read the sample claims, notice especially how they state all the facts *calmly. The writer never loses his or her temper, never makes a threat, and never attempts to place blame.* At all times, the letter is directed toward the solution.

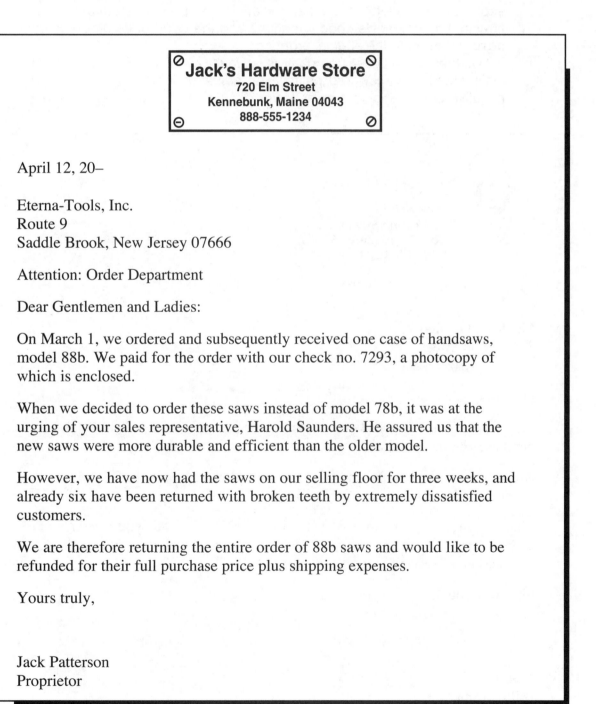

Jack's Hardware Store
720 Elm Street
Kennebunk, Maine 04043
888-555-1234

April 12, 20–

Eterna-Tools, Inc.
Route 9
Saddle Brook, New Jersey 07666

Attention: Order Department

Dear Gentlemen and Ladies:

On March 1, we ordered and subsequently received one case of handsaws, model 88b. We paid for the order with our check no. 7293, a photocopy of which is enclosed.

When we decided to order these saws instead of model 78b, it was at the urging of your sales representative, Harold Saunders. He assured us that the new saws were more durable and efficient than the older model.

However, we have now had the saws on our selling floor for three weeks, and already six have been returned with broken teeth by extremely dissatisfied customers.

We are therefore returning the entire order of 88b saws and would like to be refunded for their full purchase price plus shipping expenses.

Yours truly,

Jack Patterson
Proprietor

Figure 6–4
Claim II

Adjustments

Claims should be answered *promptly* with a letter that will restore the customer's goodwill and confidence in the company. Like a claim, a letter of *adjustment* should emphasize the solution rather than the error and convince the customer that you understand and want to be fair.

An adjustment letter should begin with a positive statement, expressing sympathy and understanding. Near the start, it should let the reader know what is being done, and this news, good or bad, should be followed by an explanation. The letter should end with another positive statement, reaffirming the company's good intentions and the value of its products but **never** referring to the original problem.

Whether or not your company is at fault, even the most belligerent claim should be answered politely. An adjustment letter should **not** be negative or suspicious; it must **never** accuse the customer or grant any

---

*G*leason's
DEPARTMENT STORE
2297 Front Street
Phoenix, Arizona 85007
(800) 555-1234

December 8, 20–

Ms. Rosetta Falco
811 Regent Street
Phoenix, Arizona 85027

Dear Ms. Falco:

As you mentioned in your letter of December 3, you were indeed billed for a purchase you had not made.

According to our records, you should not have been charged the $83.95, and the sum has been stricken from your account.

Thank you for bringing this matter to our attention. We hope you have not been inconvenienced and will visit Gleason's soon so that we may again have the pleasure of serving you.

Sincerely yours,

Xiao Li
Billing Department

Figure 6–5
Letter of Adjustment I

adjustment grudgingly. Remember, your company's image and goodwill are at stake when you respond even to unjustified claims.

When the facts of a claim have been confirmed, one of three fair solutions is possible:

1. The requested adjustment is granted.
2. A compromise adjustment is proposed.
3. Any adjustment is denied.

Responsibility for the problem, reliability of the customer, and the nature of the business relationship are all considered in determining a fair adjustment. But the ultimate settlement must always be within the bounds of *company policy*.

Granting an Adjustment

This letter should be cheerful, freely admitting errors and willingly offering the adjustment. It should express appreciation for the information provided

---

Eterna-Tools, Inc. Route 9, Saddle Brook, NJ 07666
800-555-1234

April 19, 20–

Mr. Jack Patterson
Jack's Hardware Store
720 Elm Street
Kennebunk, Maine 04043

Dear Mr. Patterson:

We are sorry that the model 88b handsaws you purchased have not lived up to your expectations. Frankly, we are surprised they have proved so fragile and appreciate your returning them to us. Our product development staff is already at work trying to discover the source of the problem.

We are glad to assume the shipping costs you incurred, Mr. Patterson. But may we suggest that, instead of a refund, you apply the price of these saws to the cost of an order of model 78b saws. Your own experience will bear out their reliability, and we are sure your customers will be pleased with an Eterna-Tool Product.

If you telephone our order department to approve the shipment, your 78b handsaws will be on their way within 24 hours.

Sincerely yours,

Davinda Mohabir
Customer Relations

Figure 6–6
Letter of Adjustment II

ATLAS PHOTOCOPIERS, INC.
810 WARREN STREET
NEW YORK, NEW YORK 10007
(800) 555-1234

August 28, 20–

Mr. Thomas Shandy
Finance Director
Handleman & Burns, Ltd.
401 Maiden Lane
New York, New York 10038

Dear Mr. Shandy:

We are sorry that you are not completely satisfied with your Atlas photo-copier. You are entirely justified in expecting more than eighteen months of reliable performance from an Atlas office machine, and we are always eager to service any product that does not for some reason live up to standards.

We appreciate your giving us the opportunity to inspect the malfunctioning copier. According to our service representative, two problems contributed to the unit's breakdown. It is apparently being used for a significantly higher volume of copying than it was built for (as indicated in both the sales material and user's manual with which you were provided). Furthermore, there are indications that the cover is not being properly closed before documents are copied. The resultant "sky-shots" can lead to the burnout of a number of mechanical parts.

Although we are not prepared to offer you a replacement copier as you suggested (indeed the one-year warrantee has been expired for six months), we would be happy to take the damaged copier as a trade-in on another, larger-capacity Atlas copier. We believe this arrangement would better meet your department's needs and be more economically advisable than additional repairs on the old unit. Please let us know if you would like to speak to a sales representative about the terms of a trade-in.

Yours truly,

Larry Tristram
Vice President Customer Service
Ext. 605

Figure 6–7
Letter of Adjustment III

in the claim. The letter *may* include an explanation of what went wrong. It *should* include an indication that similar errors will be unlikely in the future. Finally, it should *resell* the company, perhaps by suggesting future business (see Figure 6–5).

Offering a Compromise Adjustment

This letter is written when neither the company nor the customer is entirely at fault. It must express an attitude of pleasant cooperation. It should be based on facts and offer a reason for refusing the requested adjustment. As in Figure 6–6, it should immediately make a counteroffer that meets the customer halfway. Of course, it should leave the decision to accept the adjustment to the customer and suggest a course of action.

Refusing an Adjustment

Like all refusals, this adjustment letter is most difficult to write, for you must try nevertheless to rebuild your customer's goodwill. It must say no graciously but firmly while convincing the customer of the company's fairness and responsibility.

A letter refusing an adjustment should begin by expressing the customer's point of view (see Figure 6–7). It should demonstrate your sympathy and desire to be fair. It should emphasize the careful consideration the claim received.

When saying no, it is often tactful, moreover, to present the explanation *before* the decision and to include an appeal to the customer's sense of fair play. Also, an effective conclusion might suggest an alternative course of action the customer could take.

■■■■■ PRACTICE CORRESPONDENCE

The situations described in these problems call for either a claim or an adjustment letter. Prepare the appropriate letter as instructed.

A. In order to entertain and impress an important out-of-town business associate, you made dinner reservations at Club Cammarata, a prestigious restaurant known to cater to a business clientele. Your reservations were for 7:00 P.M. on June 8, and you and your guest arrived promptly. Your table, however, was not ready, and you were kept waiting for one hour and fifteen minutes. Intermittent inquiries were received by the maître d' with rude indifference. Consequently, your guest became extremely annoyed with the restaurant as well as with you. Write an appropriate complaint letter to the restaurant's owner (Enrico Cammarata, Club Cammarata, 200 Merrimack Road, Merrimack, NH 03054).

B. Refer to Exercise A and write the response that Enrico Cammarata should send to placate his dissatisfied customer and preserve his reputation in the Merrimack business community.

C. On September 5, Arnold Hayes received a monthly statement from Nayak & Nolan (1000 French Market Place, New Orleans, Louisiana 70016), where he has had a charge account for eight years. The statement included a "previous balance" from the August statement. However, Mr. Hayes had promptly paid that balance (of $81.23) on August 7 and has a canceled check to prove it. Write the claim from Mr. Hayes, 80 Arch Drive, New Orleans, Louisiana 70055, asking that his account be cleared up. Mention his enclosure of a check to cover the remaining balance on his account ($107.80).

D. Refer to Exercise C and write the letter of adjustment from Nayak & Nolan, acknowledging the error.

E. On October 7, the Kitchen Korner, 47-03 Parkway Drive, St. Paul, Minnesota 55104, placed an order for two dozen poultry shears from the Northridge Cutlery Company, 2066 Yellow Circle, Minnetonka, Minnesota 55343. By November 30, the shears have still not arrived, and there has been no letter from Northridge Cutlery explaining the delay. Write the claim from Kitchen Korner inquiring about the order. Emphasize these concerns: Did the order arrive? Why was neither an acknowledgment nor a stopgap letter sent? Will the shears arrive in time for pre-Christmas shopping?

F. Refer to Exercise E and write the letter from Northridge Cutlery answering Kitchen Korner's claim. Explain the delay as caused by a strike of local truckers. Apologize for failing to notify the customer.

7.
Sales and Public Relations Letters

All business letters are in a sense sales letters, as we have already observed. And all business letters are also public relations letters in that one must always seek to establish and maintain goodwill. But some letters are written for the express purpose of selling, and others are written for no other reason than to earn the reader's goodwill.

These letters—*sales* letters and *public relations* letters—require a highly specialized style of writing. Both demand a writer with *flair* and the ability to win the reader with words. For this reason, most large companies employ professional writers—advertising and public relations specialists—who handle all the sales and publicity writing.

Not only do advertising or public relations writers know how to appeal to people's buying motives; they know how to *find* potential buyers. They must know how to acquire mailing lists (such sources as a company's own files, telephone books, and directories are good starts) and how to select the right audience from those lists.

Nevertheless, and especially in smaller companies, there are times when almost any businessperson will have to compose either a sales letter or a public relations letter. While the nuances of style may be beyond the scope of this chapter, certain basic guidelines can help you win a desired sale or earn an associate's goodwill.

Sales Letters

Sales letters may be broken down into three categories: direct mail, retail, and promotion. While the manner of the sale is different for each, all share a common purpose—to sell a product or service.

Direct Mail Sales Letters

Direct mail, or mail order, attempts to sell directly to the customer *through the mail* (Figure 7–1). The direct mail sales letter, therefore, does the entire selling job. A salesperson never calls on the customer; the product is never even seen in person. Solely on the basis of the description and inducements in the letter, the customer is urged to buy—to mail a check and wait for his purchase to arrive.

A direct mail letter must, consequently, include a "hard sell." It must grab the reader's attention with its physical appearance; the use of flashy envelopes and the inclusion of brochures or samples often help. It must develop the reader's interest with appealing headlines and a thorough

CCS INDUSTRIES, INC.
8188 Wrigley Boulevard
Chicago, Illinois 99999
ccsi.com 800-123-4567

March 3, 20—

Dear Mr. Celaj:

Only an idiot would leave his car unlocked in a city like Chicago. Yet thousands of cars are stolen nationwide every year because drivers not only forget to lock their cars—they even leave their keys in the ignition!

We know, Mr. Celaj, that you would not ignore such a simple precaution. That's why we'd like to take this opportunity to advise you to another simple means of protecting your car—the Crookproof Cutoff Switch. Endorsed by the Midwest Auto Insurance Council and priced at just $29.95, the Crookproof Cutoff Switch can safeguard your vehicle, whether you're parked on the street or in the seeming security of your garage.

When you install a Crookproof Cutoff Switch, you make theft virtually impossible. Installation is easy with our illustrated instructions and just two basic tools. And so, because only you know where the switch is installed, you and only you can start your engine. Even a thief with a key will be stopped dead in his tracks.

The Crookproof Cutoff Switch is just $29.95 plus postage and handling. It is available only through the mail—you can't buy it in any store. And for a limited time, we will send you, a preferred customer, a set of license plate frames FREE with your purchase. These durable, eye-catching cast-alloy frames are a $19.99 value.

Ordering a Crookproof Cutoff Switch is simple. Just have a credit card ready and call our toll-free number.

1-800-123-4567

Don't delay, Mr. Celaj. Lock your car, take your keys, and install a Crookproof Cutoff Switch today. For only $29.95, you'll protect your vehicle for a long, long time.

Yours truly,

Figure 7–1
Direct Mail Sales Letter

physical description of the product; several pictures, from different angles, are a good idea.

Moreover, a direct mail letter must convince the reader of the product's quality and value. Such evidence as details and statistics, testimonies, and guarantees are essential when a customer cannot see or test a product for herself. And finally, to clinch the deal, a direct mail letter must facilitate action: clear directions for ordering plus a reply card and postage-paid envelope make buying easy; a "send-no-money-now" appeal or the offer of a premium provides additional inducement.

Retail Sales Letters

Retail sales letters (Figure 7–2) are commonly used by retail businesses to announce sales or stimulate patronage. Their advantage over other forms of advertising (such as television, radio, or newspaper ads) is that letters can be aimed selectively—at the specific audience most likely to buy. An

Justin's
Winston–Salem, NC 27106
www.anycompany.com

January 24, 20—

Dear Customer:

Now that the scaffolds are down and the hammering has stopped, you are probably aware that Justin's has opened a new store in the Bethabara Shopping Center. We are extremely proud of this gleaming new addition to the Justin's family.

To celebrate the occasion, we are having a Grand Opening Sale, and every Justin's store will be in on it.

EVERYTHING in ALL our stores will be marked down 10–30%. Designer jeans that were $60–$90 are now $40–$60. An assortment of 100% silk blouses, originally $60–$95, are on sale for $40–$65. The savings are incredible.

The sale is for one day only, January 31. But the doors will open at 9 A.M., so you can shop early for the best selection. And, of course, your Justin's and VISA cards are always welcome.

Sincerely yours,

Justin Olsen
President

Figure 7–2
Retail Sales Letter

electronics store, for example, holding a sale on electronic phone books and digital diaries, could target letters specifically to businesspeople and professionals as opposed to, say, homemakers or educators, thus reaching customers with the clearest need for the product.

A letter announcing a sale must contain certain information:

1. the reason for the sale (a seasonal clearance, holiday, special purchase, etc.);
2. the dates on which the sale will take place;
3. an honest description of the sale merchandise (including a statement of what is and is not marked down);
4. comparative prices (original price versus sale price or approximate markdown percentages);
5. a statement encouraging the customer to act fast.

Sales Promotion Letters

A sales promotion letter (Figure 7–3) solicits interest rather than an immediate sale. It is written to encourage inquiries rather than orders. A product that requires demonstration or elaborate explanation, for example, could be introduced in a promotional letter; interested customers will inquire further. Similarly, products requiring elaborate and expensive descriptive material (for example, a large brochure or sample) could be introduced in a promotional letter; uninterested names on a mailing list would then be screened out, leaving only serious potential customers and thereby cutting costs.

Like other sales letters, a promotional letter must stimulate the reader's interest and describe the product. But it need not be as detailed: customers desiring further information are invited to send in a reply card, contact a sales representative, or visit a web site. Of course, such inquiries **must** be answered promptly by either a salesperson or a letter. And the follow-up letter (which could include a leaflet or sample) should provide complete information, including specific answers to questions the customer may have asked. The follow-up attempts to convince the reader to buy and tells how to make the purchase.

All of the sales letters described in this chapter have certain features in common: they convey *enthusiasm* for the product and employ *evocative language*. They demonstrate the writer's knowledge of both product and customer. And they illustrate the advertising principles known as AIDA:

1. *A*ttention: The letter opens with a gimmick to grab the reader's attention and create the desire to know more.
2. *I*nterest: The letter provides information and plays up certain features of the product to build the reader's interest.
3. *D*esire: The sales pitch appeals to one or more personal needs (such as prestige, status, comfort, safety, or money) to stimulate the reader's desire.
4. *A*ction: The letter makes it easy for the reader to buy and encourages immediate action.

Smith & Marcus

Financial Consultants

9732 Commonwealth Avenue

Boston, Massachusetts 02215

February 10, 20—

Dear

In times of economic uncertainty, personal financial planning can pose more challenges than running your own business. Determining the investment vehicles that will protect your own and your family's future requires financial insight and information.

That is why many successful business owners like yourself have engaged the services of the personal financial consultants at Smith & Marcus. We have both the expertise and objectivity to help you sort out your long- and short-term financial goals and then select the investment strategies that will meet those goals. Whether your immediate concerns are tax planning or estate planning, we believe we have the answers to your financial questions.

To introduce you to the sort of answers we have, you are cordially invited to a seminar, "What a Personal Financial Planner Can Do for You." The seminar will take place on Wednesday, March 1, 20—, at 7 P.M. in the Essex Room of the Essex–Marlboro Hotel. Because seats are limited, we would appreciate your letting us know if you plan to attend by telephoning Dorothy Phillips at 555-1234, extension 222.

Yours truly,

Alex Smith

Figure 7–3
Sales Promotion Letter

Public Relations Letters

Public relations concerns the efforts a company makes to influence public opinion, to create a favorable company image. Its purpose is **not** to make a sale or stimulate immediate business, but rather to convey to the public such positive qualities as the company's fair-mindedness, reliability, or efficiency.

Public relations is big business, and large corporations spend millions of dollars a year on their public relations campaigns. When a major oil company sponsors a program on public television, that is public relations; when a large chemical company establishes a college scholarship fund, that is public relations, too.

Public relations specialists know how to use all the mass media (television, radio, magazines, newspapers, films, and the Internet); they know how to compose press releases and set up press conferences, prepare broadcast announcements, and arrange public receptions.

But public relations exists on a smaller scale as well. It is the local butcher's remembering a shopper's name, and it is a local hardware store's buying T-shirts for the Little League. Basically, public relations is the attempt to establish and maintain **goodwill**.

Pine & White

5050 Masssachusetts Avenue
Boston, Massachusetts 02116
1-800-555-1234

June 12, 20–

Ms. Beverly May
150 Glen Terrace
Needham, Massachusetts 02492

Dear Ms. May:

Now that you've used your Pine & White credit card for the very first time, we are sure you have seen for yourself the convenience and ease a charge account provides. So we won't try to "resell" you on all the benefits you can take advantage of as a new charge customer.

We'd simply like to take this time to thank you for making your first charge purchase and assure you that everyone at Pine & White is always ready to serve you. We are looking forward to a long and mutually rewarding association.

Welcome to the "family."

Sincerely yours,

Christine Popoulos
Customer Relations

Figure 7–4
Public Relations Letter I

Public relations letters, therefore, are those letters written for the purpose of strengthening goodwill. Some of these can be considered *social business letters* (see Chapter 8), such as invitations, thank-you notes, and letters of congratulations. Others are similar to advertising, such as announcements of openings or changes in store facilities or policies. Still others are simply friendly gestures, such as a note welcoming a new charge customer or thanking a new customer for her first purchase (Figure 7–4).

**5050 Masssachusetts Avenue
Boston, Massachusetts 02116**
1-800-555-1234

May 26, 20–

Mrs. Addison Tanghal
224 East Elm Street
Brookline, Massachusetts 02445

Dear Mrs. Tanghal:

It's been more than six months since you charged a purchase at Pine & White, and we can't help worrying that we've done something to offend you. We are sure you are aware of the convenience and ease your charge account provides, but we would like to assure you once again that everyone at Pine & White is always ready to serve you.

If you have encountered a problem with our service or merchandise, we want to know. It is our sincere desire to give you the personal attention and satisfaction you have come over the years to expect from Pine & White. And we welcome the advice of our customers and friends to keep us on our toes.

Please fill out the enclosed reply card if something has been troubling you. We will give your comments immediate attention, as we look forward to seeing you once again at our Brookline store and all our other branches.

Sincerely,

Christine Popoulos
Customer Relations

Figure 7–5
Public Relations Letter II

MURGANO TRAVEL
1123 North Union Street
Montgomery, Alabama 36104
(800) 555-1234 *www.anycompany.com*

February 26, 20–

Dear

Most business travelers these days acknowledge that travel, particularly outside U.S. borders, is fraught with more anxiety than ever before. In our post-9/11 world, even regions as stable as western Europe can harbor danger. Just ask the tourists evacuated from Sacre Coeur last month! At Murgano Travel, we believe our responsibility to you does not stop with confirmed reservations and itineraries. Your safety when you travel is also our deep concern.

We know that, as a business traveler, you cannot always avoid political hot spots. Therefore, our first recommendation is that you always consult two travel advisory web sites before you go:

U.S. State Department advisories (*travel.state.gov*)
U.K. Foreign & Commonwealth Office advisories (*fco.gov.uk*)

In addition to getting these two perspectives on the safety of your destination, we also suggest these do's and don'ts:

Do take an international cell phone.
Don't use public transportation or hail a taxi on the street. Have your hotel arrange transportation.
Do carry a photocopy of your passport. Leave the original in your hotel safe.
Don't wear religious jewelry or clothing with American logos.
Do keep up with world events on CNN or BBCWorldNews.
Don't attend large public events (athletic as well as political). Avoid crowds.
Do carry your hotel's business card as a quick way to communicate with a non-English-speaking driver or police officer.
Don't photograph sensitive sites such as airports, government buildings, or crowds.

Finally, our basic advice is simple: **Use common sense, err on the side of caution**, and **keep your wits about you**. And, be confident that, having trusted us at Murgano to take care of all your travel arrangements, we are also *here* should you need us when you're *there*.

Sincerely,

Maria Murgano

Figure 7–6
Public Relations Letter III

A specific kind of public relations letter is designed to demonstrate a company's interest in its customers. This letter (Figure 7–5) is written *inviting* complaints. Its purpose is to discover causes of customer dissatisfaction before they become too serious. (Responses to such letters must always get a prompt follow-up to assure the customer that the reported problem will be looked into.)

Similarly, to forestall complaints (and of course encourage business), large companies frequently send *informative* letters that *educate* the public (Figure 7–6). For example, a supplier of gas and electricity may include an explanation of new higher rates with the monthly bill. Or a telephone company will enclose a fact sheet on ways to save money on long-distance calls.

Whatever the main purpose for a public relations letter—to establish, maintain, or even revive business—remember that *all* public relations letters must be *friendly*. Their real purpose is to create a friend for the company.

■■■■■ PRACTICE CORRESPONDENCE

On another sheet of paper, prepare either a sales or public relations letter as called for in each of the following situations.

A. Select a product (such as electronic gadgets, magazines, or cosmetics) that you have considered purchasing (or have actually purchased) by mail. Write a letter that could be used to stimulate direct mail sales for the product.

B. Geoffrey's, a fine men's clothing store located at 600 Arlington Street, Boston, Massachusetts 02116, is having its annual fall clearance sale. All summer and selected fall merchandise will be on sale with discounts up to 60% on some items. The sale will begin on September 10. Write a letter to be sent to all charge customers, inviting them to attend three presale days, September 7–9, during which they will find a full selection of sale merchandise before it is advertised to the public.

C. You work for the ABC Corporation, Fort Madison, Iowa 52622, manufacturer of educational software. Write a letter to be sent to the heads of all business schools in the area, inviting them to inquire about your latest software packages. Describe some of the program's special features and tell the reader how to receive additional information.

D. You are employed by the First National Bank of Dayton, 1742 Broad Street, Dayton, Ohio 45463. You recently opened both a savings and a checking account for Claire Paulsen, a new resident of Dayton. Write a letter to Ms. Paulsen (2222 Elm Street, Dayton, Ohio 45466) to welcome her to the city and to the bank.

E. Imagine that you work in the customer relations department of a large furniture store. Write a letter that could be sent to customers who have bought furniture for one room of their home, encouraging them to buy furniture for another room. Remind them of the quality and service they received when they did business with you in the past. Urge them to shop with you again.

8.
Social Business Letters

Like public relations letters, social business correspondence does not promote immediate business. Yet an astute businessperson will recognize the writing of a letter of congratulations or appreciation as a fertile chance to build goodwill.

The occasions that call for social business letters are many; such letters may express congratulations, sympathy, or thanks, or may convey an invitation or announcement. These messages may be extended to friends and personal acquaintances, to coworkers and employees, and to business associates. They may even be sent to persons who are unknown to the writer but who represent potential customers.

While the *tone* of a social business letter will vary with the relationship between the correspondents, all such lettters must sound **sincere**. And, with the possible exception of an announcement, they should avoid any hint of a sales pitch.

Social business letters are often written on smaller stationery than letterhead. Some may be handwritten or formally engraved, rather than typed. Moreover, as an additional personalized touch, the salutation in a social business letter may be followed by a comma instead of a colon.

Because the language of a social business letter must strike a delicate balance between the personal and professional, the friendly and formal, it is a good idea to refer to a current book of etiquette for proper wording. Such a reference work will serve as a reliable guide, especially when composing formal invitations and letters of condolence.

Letters of Congratulations

A letter of congratulations builds goodwill by stroking the reader's ego: everyone likes to have accomplishments acknowledged.

The occasions for congratulatory messages are numerous: promotions (Figure 8–1); appointments, and elections; achievements, awards, and honors; marriages and births (Figure 8–2); anniversaries and retirements.

Whether written to a close friend or a distant business associate, any letter of congratulations must be **sincere** and **enthusiastic**. It may be short, but it should contain **personal** remarks or references.

A letter of congratulations should include three essential ingredients; it should:

1. begin with the expression of congratulations;
2. mention the reason for the congratulations with a personal or informal twist;

Dear Alan,

Congratulations on your promotion to senior accounts executive. You have worked hard for Rembow Consultants, and I am delighted that your efforts have been rewarded.

As you move into your new office and assume the weight of responsibilities that go along with your new position, please let me know if I can be of any assistance.

Sincerely,

Figure 8–1
Letter of Congratulations I

Ruth T. Travis
1156 Clearview Avenue
Cold Spring Harbor, New York, 11724

Dear Monica,
    Congratulations on the birth of your grandchild, David Gary. You and Jim must be thrilled by the experience of becoming grandparents.
    Please extend my warmest wishes to your daughter Jane and her husband. May this new addition to your family bring you all joy.
                    Sincerely,
                    Ruth

Figure 8–2
Letter of Congratulations II

3. end with an expression of goodwill (such as praise or confidence—**never** say "Good luck," which implies chance rather than achievement).

Letters of Condolence

When an acquaintance experiences the death of a loved one, it is proper, although difficult, to send a message of condolence (see Figures 8–3 and 8–4). To avoid awkwardness, many people opt for commercially printed sympathy cards, but a specially written note is more **personal** and **genuine**.

A message of condolence lets your reader know that you are aware of his personal grief and wish to lend sympathy and support. The message, therefore, should be **simple**, **honest**, and **direct**, and it should express **sorrow** with **dignity** and **respect**. (The expression "I am sorry," however, should be avoided, for as a cliché it sounds flat and insincere.)

The message of condolence should begin by referring to the situation and the people involved. This should be a bland statement that avoids unpleasant reminders. The note may use the word *death* but should **not** describe the death.

The rest of the note should be brief: an encouraging reference to the future (which should be uplifting but realistic), or, if appropriate, a gesture of goodwill (such as an offer of help).

> **Note:** A letter of sympathy is also sent to someone who is ill or who has suffered an accident or other misfortune.

Dear Mr. Summers,

I would like to extend the deep sympathy of all of us at Jason Associates.

We had the privilege of knowing and working with Edith for many years, and her friendly presence will be sadly missed.

Please consider us your friends and telephone us if we can be of any help.

Sincerely,

Figure 8–3
Letter of Condolence I

Michael Barrett
4368-83 Street, Brooklyn, New York 11214

Dear Hal,

Roseann and I were deeply saddened to learn of your great loss. We hope the love you and Edith shared will help comfort you in the days ahead.

If there is anything we can do for you now or in the future, please let us know.

With much sympathy,
Michael

Figure 8–4
Letter of Condolence II

Letters of Appreciation

In business, as in life, it is important to say "thank you."

We have already seen (see Chapter 7) that letters of appreciation should be sent to new customers upon the opening of an account or the making of a first purchase. But many other occasions call for a "thank you" as well; a note of appreciation should always be sent after receiving

1. gifts
2. favors
3. courtesies
4. hospitality
5. donations

A note of thanks should also be sent in response to a letter of congratulations.

A thank-you note may be **brief**, but it must be **prompt**, for it must, like all social business letters, sound **sincere**.

A proper letter of appreciation (see Figures 8–5 and 8–6) will contain three key elements; it will:

1. begin by saying "thank you";
2. make a sincere personal comment;
3. end with a positive and genuine statement (**never** say "Thank you again").

Dear Mr. Yoshimura,

Thank you very much for referring Natalie Slate to us. We are, of course, pleased to take on a new client. But even more, we appreciate your confidence in our legal services and your willingness to communicate this confidence to others.

Be assured that we will continue to make every effort to live up to your expectations.

Cordially,

Figure 8–5
Letter of Appreciation I

Lisa Longo
9 Nutmeg Lane
Framingham, Massachusetts 01702

Dear Lucy,

Thank you for the beautiful paperweight. As it sits on my desk, I shall always be reminded of your valuable support when I was up for promotion.

Sincerely,
Lisa

Figure 8–6
Letter of Appreciation II

Invitations

While such events as openings, previews, and demonstrations may be advertised in newspapers or on handbills, guests may be more carefully selected if invitations are sent by letter.

Formal events, such as a reception, open house, or formal social gathering, *require* formal invitations. These invitations can be engraved or printed, or they can be handwritten on note-size stationery.

A general invitation (Figure 8–8) should be cordial and sincere; a formal invitation (Figure 8–7) should be less personal, written in the third person. Either kind of invitation, however, must do three things:

1. invite the reader to the gathering;
2. offer a reason for the gathering;
3. give the date, time, and place of the gathering.

A formal invitation should, in addition, include an R.S.V.P. notation. This abbreviation stands for *répondez s'il vous plaît;* it asks the reader to please respond, that is, "Please let us know if you plan to attend." Alternatively, the notation "Regrets Only" may be used, asking only those who **cannot** attend to notify the host in advance.

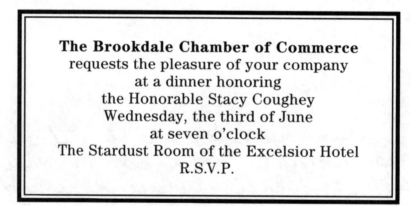

The Brookdale Chamber of Commerce
requests the pleasure of your company
at a dinner honoring
the Honorable Stacy Coughey
Wednesday, the third of June
at seven o'clock
The Stardust Room of the Excelsior Hotel
R.S.V.P.

Figure 8–7
Invitation I

Jaco Films, Inc.

9120 Avenue of the Americas, New York, New York 10036

800-123-4567 *www.anycompany.com*

January 3, 20—

Dear

In a few weeks, JACO will proudly release its new feature-length film, *The Purchase*, starring Amanda Theriot in her first appearance in seventeen years.

A special preview showing of *The Purchase*, for friends of Ms. Theriot and of JACO Films, will be held on January 19, at 8 P.M., at the Regent Theater on Broadway and 52nd Street.

You are cordially invited to attend this preview. Admission will be by ticket only, which you will find enclosed. Following the film, refreshments will be served.

Sincerely yours,

Georgia Stringfellow
Assistant to the Producer

Figure 8–8
Invitation II

Announcements

Announcements may rightly be considered closer to public relations than social business letters. They may take the form of news releases, advertisements, or promotional letters. But *formal announcements* resemble invitations in both tone and format. Indeed, the combination formal announcement/invitation (Figure 8–10) is not an uncommon form of correspondence.

Business events such as openings (see Figure 8–9), mergers, and promotions (see Figure 8–11) may be the subject of both formal and informal announcements.

Dr. Richard Levine
announces the opening of his office
for the practice of pediatric medicine
1420 North Grand Street
Suite 1B
Miami, Florida 33133
(402) 555-1234

Figure 8–9
Formal Announcement

The ALDO Corporation
is pleased to announce the appointment of
Ms. Firuz Darkhosh
as its new executive vice-president
and requests the pleasure of your company
at a reception in her honor
Friday, the twelfth of April
at four o'clock
The President's Suite Room 510

Figure 8–10
Combination Announcement/Invitation

TO: All Personnel

FROM: George Hart, President

DATE: April 3, 20—

SUBJECT: The New Executive Vice-President

We are please to announce the appointment of Ms. Firuz Darkhosh to the position of executive vice-president.

Ms. Darkhosh has been with ALDO for eight years, first as assistant manager of marketing and then, for the past five years, as manager of marketing. She attended Baruch College and Pace University, where she earned a master's degree in business administration.

I'm sure you will all join me in extending hearty congratulations to Ms. Darkhosh and best wishes for her future here at ALDO.

GH

Figure 8–11
Informal Announcement

▬▬▬ PRACTICE CORRESPONDENCE

For each of the social situations described, prepare a correspondence that is appropriate to business relationships.

A. You are administrative assistant to the president of Burton and Doyle, Inc., 355 Bond Street, Oshkosh, Wisconsin 54901. Your boss, Mr. Arthur J. Burton, asks you to write a letter of congratulations, which he will sign, to Theodore Manning, 72 North Eden, La Crosse, Wisconsin 54601, a junior executive who has just been named "Father of the Year" by the La Crosse Boy Scouts Council.

B. You are employed by American Associates, Inc., 28 North Howard Street, Philadelphia, Pennsylvania 19122. Your boss, Jacqueline Austin, 4500 Poplar Street, Hanover, Pennsylvania 17331, has not been in the office for several days, and it has just been announced that her mother died. Since Ms. Austin will not be returning to work for a week or two, write a letter to express your condolence.

C. You have worked for the law firm of Lederer, Lederer and Hall, 807 East 23 Street, New York, New York 10010, for many years. On the occasion of your tenth anniversary with the company, an office party was held in your honor, and Mr. Gerald Hall presented you with a wristwatch as a token of the company's appreciation. Write a letter to Mr. Hall thanking him and the entire company for the party and the gift.

D. The Merchants Insurance Company of Tucson is holding its annual executive banquet on September 8, at 7 P.M. It will be held in the Gold Room of the Barclay Country Club, 7000 Country Club Road, Tucson, Arizona 85726. Design a *formal* invitation that the company can send to all its executives. Include a request for response by August 24th.

E. A baby, Angela May, has been born to Mr. and Mrs. Andrew Lopato. She was born at Community General Hospital on February 9 at 7 A.M. and weighed seven pounds seven ounces. Prepare a *formal* announcement that the Lopatos could use to inform friends and business associates of Angela's birth.

9.
Employment Correspondence

Of all the different kinds of letters this book discusses, perhaps none are more important for your personal career than those letters you write to apply for a job. Your letter of application and accompanying résumé, if well planned and written, can do much to help you secure the job of your choice.

Before you can write your résumé or prepare a cover letter, you must do some thinking about yourself, for your employment correspondence must present a prospective employer with a favorable—and desirable— picture of your personality, background, and experiences.

A good way to start is to make a list. In any order, as you think of them, list such facts as:

Jobs you have held
Schools you have gone to
Areas you have majored in
Special courses you have taken
Extracurricular activities you have joined in
Memberships you have held
Awards or honors you have received
Athletics you enjoy
Languages you speak
Special interests you have
Special skills you have

Try to include on your list any **fact** that could help an employer see your *value* as an employee.

After you are satisfied with your list, rewrite it, arranging the facts into categories. This will serve as your worksheet when you are ready to write your résumé and letter of application.

The Résumé

The *résumé* is an **outline** of all you have to offer a prospective employer (see Figures 9–1, 9–2, 9–3, and 9–4). It is a presentation of your qualifications, your background, and your experiences arranged in such a way as to convince a businessperson to grant you an interview.

Your résumé, with its cover letter, is the first impression you make on an employer. For that reason, it must look **professional** and exemplify those traits you want the employer to believe you possess.

First of all, a résumé *must* be **printed** on business-size bond. It is acceptable to send photocopies, but these must be **perfect** and look like originals. This can be accomplished by using the services of a quick print

Olga Godunov
392 Eagle Street
Terre Haute, Indiana 47807
111-555-1234

CAREER OBJECTIVE:
To obtain a position as an executive secretary with a large corporation.

WORK EXPERIENCE:

March 2003 to Present	Secretary, The Benlow Corporation, Terre Haute, Indiana

General running of the office of a small private firm; duties included preparing correspondence, filing, billing, answering telephones, scheduling appointments, etc. Demonstrated ability to handle multiple tasks simultaneously.

October 2001 to March 2003	Receptionist, Dr. Mark Roan, Berne, Indiana

First tier of customer service: interacted with clients in person and on telephones; evaluated incoming calls and directed them to appropriate personnel; reorganized reception area to provide visitors with more positive first experience with the company. Demonstrated strong communications skills and tact when dealing with challenging people.

January 2001 to October 2001	File Clerk, Ajax Insurance Company, Berne, Indiana

Reorganized and streamlined file system; initiated switch over to computer-based file system. Proven quick learner with ability to organize large quantities of data.

EDUCATION:
Judson Secretarial School, Berne, Indiana. September 1999–January 2001. Courses in typing, filing, bookkeeping, and business machines operation.

Completed company-offered professional development courses: Assertiveness Skills; Sexual Harassment; Security Awareness; Microsoft Word

SPECIAL SKILLS:
Typing–70 w.p.m.
Languages–French
Computers–WordPerfect. Microsoft Word. QYX Level IV

Figure 9–1
Résumé I

Arnold O'Connor
212 Lakeview Drive
Duluth, Minnesota 34377
111-555-1234

Career Objective
An entry level position as a physician assistant

Education
Minnesota State University, St. Paul
Bachelor of Science degree, June 2012
Major: Physician Assistant Program
Courses included: Clinical Medicine, Medical Assessment, Geriatric
    Medicine, Pediatric Medicine, as well as Business Management and
    Psychology
Hospital rotations included: Emergency Medicine, Orthopedics, Pediatrics,
    and Geriatrics

Duluth Central High School, Duluth
Diploma, June 2008
Graduation Award: Senior Prize in Biology

Work Experience
Physician Assistant Residency, Pediatrics Department
    Downstate General Hospital
    Rochester, Minnesota
    September 2011–May 2012
    Observed and assisted doctors and physician assistant during patient
    examinations, test result interpretation, and illness diagnosis

Office Assistant, Office of Grete Svensen, MD
    Duluth, Minnesota
    July 2007–August 2008
    Answered telephones, scheduled patient appointments, assisted with
    general office procedures

Skills
Language: French

Licenses
Licensed Physician Assistant, June 2012

Figure 9–2
Résumé II

Nicolas Balaj
201 New Oak Street
Newark, New Jersey 07102
111-555-1234
nicb@s&s.com

CAREER OBJECTIVE
Sales Management: a position utilizing experience in sales and supervision

SKILLS
• Over 13 years in sales and sales management
• Documented success developing both leads and long-term business relationships
• Experience developing "team" environment, training and motivating sales staff

WORK EXPERIENCE
Summit & Storch   Sales Supervisor
Newark, New Jersey   2005–Present
• Supervise staff of 12 salespeople: hire and train new representatives, set quotas,
  assign leads, manage budgets, plan presentations
• Increased sales from $350,000 to $1,100,000; directed opening of southern
  office (Atlanta, Georgia); established relationships with major manufacturers
  (including Whirlpool, Maytag, and General Electric)

S.G. Walters   Sales Representative
Trenton, New Jersey   2000–2005
• Conducted sales of wide product line to major distributors in tri-state region
• Participated in product development and presentation planning
• Increased territory sales by 75%

EDUCATION

Rutgers University   B.A.–Marketing
Rutgers, New Jersey   2000

MISCELLANEOUS

• Fluent in Spanish
• Member SRBA since 2001
• Willing to travel or relocate

Figure 9–3
Résumé III

VITA GUTIERREZ
273 Cedar Street
Greenvale, NY 10548
(123) 555-1234
vitag@GUH.com

CAREER OBJECTIVE
Directorial position of a pharmacy department in a teaching hospital

EXPERIENCE
Greenvale University Hospital, Greenvale, NY

Pharmacy Supervisor   2005–present
Developed familiarity with up-to-date pharmacy-based computer systems; worked collaboratively with medical staff; participated in orientation, training, and professional development of pharmacy staff; assisted director with budgeting, purchasing, and procurement planning.

St. John's Medical Center, Peekskill, NY

Assistant Pharmacy Supervisor   2003–2005
Supervised night-shift staff; worked with critical care patients; gained experience in investigational drug services.

Staff Pharmacist   2001–2003
Became familiar with computerized and automated unit dose drug distribution and comprehensive IV admixture services; worked with pediatric, cardiac, and surgery patients.

EDUCATION & TRAINING
Albany University Hospital ASHP residency program   2000–2001
S.U.N.Y. at Albany, Albany, NY
    M.S. in Hospital Pharmacy Administration   2000
Highland College, Highland, MA
    B.S. in Pharmacy   1998

CREDENTIALS
NYS Pharmacy License, 2000
Certificate, Course in Bioterrorism Preparedness, 2001

Figure 9–4
Résumé IV

shop where your résumé can be professionally copied on bond paper. When your résumé is updated and you add new experiences, you must **reprint** the whole thing. *Never* send a résumé with handwritten, or even typed, additions squeezed in. This looks careless, unorganized, and lazy.

It is advisable to save your résumé electronically so you can update it easily and modify it to target a particular job or company. Just remember to print it on high-quality paper.

The résumé must have an overall **neat** appearance: margins should be wide and balanced. Headings should stand out (for example, be under-lined, capitalized, or printed in boldface type) and should be **parallel**.

The information contained on your résumé must be **accurate** and **complete**. It should consist of **facts**. (You will be able to *interpret* the facts in your application letter.) Because you are presenting these facts in *outline form*, the information is expressed in short phrases and industry-specific keywords rather than whole sentences.

Nowadays, it is preferable to keep a résumé to *one or two pages*. Therefore, you must be efficient in selecting the facts to include and clever in arranging them. Remember that, even with several years of var-ied experience, you are providing an outline of your work history, not an autobiography.

Working from your casual list, decide which facts you would like an employer to know. (Eliminate those you would rather he not know.) Also, consider what the employer would like to know about you. (Eliminate those facts that he would probably consider irrelevant.) Unless relevant to the job at hand, omit your religious or political affiliations. Definitely exclude negative information such as lawsuits. **Do not** offer reasons for leaving previous jobs. **Do not** make critical comments about a previous employer (on your résumé or at an interview)! And, of course, do **not** lie!

In making these decisions, keep in mind the specific job for which you are applying. What facts on your list best qualify you for the job? *These* are the facts to emphasize on your résumé.

Having narrowed down your list, recopy it—arrange the facts into logi-cal order.

Now you are ready to set up your résumé. At the top, print your name, home address, e-mail address, and telephone numbers (including your cell phone number). This information can be centered or blocked along the left margin. In either case, it provides a sufficient heading. (The word *résumé* is unnecessary.)

The rest of the résumé consists of the facts from your list, categorized and printed under headings. Some recommended headings are:

> Employment (or Career) Objective
> Education and/or Training
> Achievements and/or Accomplishments
> Awards and Honors
> Work Experience
> Related or Extracurricular Activities
> Special Skills
> Personal Data
> References

You need not use all of these categories; use, of course, only those that relate to facts on your list. Also, the order in which you list the categories is flexible. You may list your strongest sections first, or you may list first the section that is most relevant to the job in question.

For example, if you have had little business experience but are thoroughly trained, list **education** first. On the other hand, if your college education was in an unrelated field but you have had relevant part-time jobs, list **work experience** first.

Format Options

There are basically three ways to format your résumé. The one preferred by most employers, hiring managers, and recruiters is the **reverse chronological résumé**, on which you list your work experience job by job, starting with your current (or most recent) position and working backward. This provides the prospective employer with a full picture of your background. It eliminates any suspicion of an erratic or sporadic work history.

On the other hand, a **functional résumé** can be effective when you do want to camouflage a weakness in your job history. If you:

> have changed jobs frequently;
> have been unemployed;
> have been self-employed, freelancing, or consulting;
> are entering the workforce for the first time;
> are returning to work after an illness;
> are returning to work after raising children

then you want to emphasize your skills while deemphasizing your sketchy experience. If you are changing careers, a **functional résumé** allows you to draw attention to those skills you acquired in your old field that will be valuable in your new one.

To set up a **functional résumé**, your planning list should focus on the tasks, duties, skills, accomplishments, and responsibilities you have performed in the past. These are your "functions." The ones that are especially relevant to the job you are seeking will serve as the headings on your résumé. Under each heading, you will elaborate the details and scope of each function you've performed and mention examples of where you performed it.

The third format option is a combination **functional/chronological résumé**. It is essentially a functional résumé with a brief outline of your work history at the end. It offers the advantages of a functional résumé but avoids any suspicion that you might be hiding something about your past.

Now let's look at the headings you will be using, whatever format you opt for.

EMPLOYMENT OBJECTIVE: Many career counselors recommend that this be included and listed first, immediately after your name and address. Mentioning a clearly defined job goal creates the favorable impression that you are a well-directed, motivated individual. On the other hand, many businesspeople prefer applicants with flexible objectives. Thus, you might consider under this heading a general statement such as, "Acceptance in a management training program" or "Entry-level position in an accounting environment."

EDUCATION List, in reverse chronological order, the schools you have attended, with school names, dates of attendance, and degrees or diplomas awarded. (Omit high school unless your high school experiences are relevant to the job being applied for or if you have no other training.) Note any job-related courses you took at each school listed. (If you attended a school but did not graduate, be sure to list relevant courses taken there.)

Also include all other education you have received—technical or career training, professional development seminars, continuing education classes, on-the-job workshops, etc.

WORK EXPERIENCE: Between WORK EXPERIENCE and EDUCATION, you should account for *all* your time since finishing school. Part-time and summer jobs, as well as volunteer work and internships, should be included. (You needn't have gotten paid to have developed a valuable and marketable skill.)

Each job experience should be listed (again, with the most recent job first) with your position or title, employer's name and location, dates of employment, and a brief description of your responsibilities. (If you have formal job descriptions or performance evaluations from your old jobs, these will give you some ideas along with industry "buzzwords" or jargon you could include.) Also include anything you accomplished that went beyond what was required (thus showing a prospective employer how enthusiastic, dedicated, and valuable you will be).

If you want to conceal gaps in your work history or, on a positive note, if your work history is very long, consider calling this section RELATED WORK EXPERIENCE, implying that you are only listing *relevant* jobs.

> **Note:** If you have been in the armed services, this may be included under WORK EXPERIENCE or a separate heading. Be sure to list the branch of the military, dates, special duties, and highest rank held.

ACHIEVEMENTS AND ACCOMPLISHMENTS, EXTRACURRICULAR ACTIVITIES, and SPECIAL SKILLS: Under these headings you may list any facts that don't fit under EDUCATION or WORK EXPERIENCE but that demonstrate an important aspect of your value to an employer. For example, if you are familiar with a particular account's software but have never worked in an accounting department, here is the place to list your knowledge. If you can operate specialized machinery or speak a foreign language, note these facts. If you hold job-related licenses or certifications, have received any grants or awards, or have written any publications, include them here as well.

Similarly, if you were treasurer of an after-school club, your experience handling money and specific duties that you performed are all important to mention. Indeed, all such memberships and activities are worth noting, for they help draw a picture of a vital, well-rounded individual.

PERSONAL DATA: Essential **facts**, such as any licenses or certifications you hold, should be included on a résumé. On the other hand, it is not necessary to list such facts as age, height, weight, health, and marital status. Indeed, **federal** and many **state laws** prohibit employers from asking about race, religion, or sex. Therefore some career counselors advise omitting this category altogether.

However, if a personal fact is particularly relevant to the job you are seeking, it may be worth mentioning (though using a heading such as MISCELLANEOUS may be better than PERSONAL DATA). For example, having a family member employed in the field could indicate that you have a thorough understanding of the responsibilities, as well as advantages and disadvantages, of the job; or being in perfect health could be important on a job that requires a great deal of physical activity or even long or irregular hours.

REFERENCES: Traditionally, the *last* section of your résumé was a list of those people willing to vouch for your ability and experience, but nowadays this should be included only if asked for. Nevertheless, even if you are **not** including a list of references on your résumé, you **should** have the list prepared. Keep it separately, ready to be taken to interviews. Former employers and teachers (especially teachers of job-related courses) are the best references. Friends or members of the clergy may be used as *character* references, but their word regarding your skills will have little weight. Each reference should be listed by name, position or title, business address, telephone number, and e-mail address. A minimum of three names is recommended.

> **Note:** Be sure to ask permission of each individual before you list anyone as a reference. Also, while some employers prefer to contact your references directly, it is a good idea to get a general letter of reference from each to keep for your own files. (Businesses move or go bankrupt; people move, retire, or die; and, after many years, you may simply have been forgotten!)

A WORD ABOUT PROFESSIONAL RÉSUMÉ WRITERS

Recent years have seen a proliferation of professional résumé services, people who will (for a fee) prepare your résumé and cover letter. Services range from simply formatting and then printing a résumé you have composed yourself to interviewing you in depth, analyzing your skills, and then composing and printing your résumé for you. Some services will even do a mass mailing.

These services are valuable if you have difficulty organizing your career data. If the service includes an interview, it can help you begin thinking of your skills in new and creative ways. Good professional résumé writers will know how to highlight your strengths and downplay your weaknesses. They can offer advice about the job hunt, interviewing, and even salary negotiations. And, of course, they are expert at both writing and designing your résumé. The downside of using a professional résumé preparer, however, is that your résumé will look just that—professionally prepared! Having obviously paid someone else to prepare your résumé can create doubts in a prospective employer's mind about your own skills, particularly if your target job calls for organizational, communication, clerical, or computer skills. If you hire a professional résumé writer, be sure your résumé ends up sounding like *you*. And be sure the professional you hire is certified, either a Nationally Certified Résumé Writer (NCRW) or a Certified Professional Résumé Writer (CPRW).

An alternative approach could be to prepare your résumé on a computer yourself. Software packages are now available that provide templates, allowing you to plug your own data into a variety of formats, simplifying the process of arranging your information as well as printing perfect copies.

Such software also requires caution, however. Be sure to delete headings that obviously don't apply to your background and to rephrase terminology that sounds "packaged," artificial, or irrelevant.

Electronic Résumés

Online job recruitment is a growing phenomenon. Therefore, it is advisable to have ready not only a paper résumé but also an **electronic résumé**, of which there are two kinds.

SCANNABLE RÉSUMÉS: When you mail or fax your paper résumé to a possible employer, that company may scan it to save in a computerized tracking system. So you must be sure your résumé is scannable.

Do use high-quality, light-colored paper.
Do not fold it.
Do not staple it.
Do not use fonts larger than 20-point-type for headings.
Do not use fonts smaller than 9 points or larger than 12 points for text.
Do not use decorative fonts for headings or for text.
Do not use underlining.
Do use white space to indicate sections.
Do use solid bullets (see Figure 9–3) to highlight key facts.

E-MAILABLE RÉSUMÉS: To e-mail a résumé, you must create a generic computer file specific for the purpose. Use a generic ASCII text file that will save your document without formatting codes. With just text (no fonts, no graphics), it will be readable by any word-processing software. You can then send it two ways:

1. e-mail it directly to the company;
2. post it on the Internet (at a company's web site, to a job bank in response to an online job posting, or to a news group).

> **An Important Tip:** You must be sure to sprinkle either type of résumé with industry terminology or "keywords" to be sure someone will actually read it. Recruiters and hiring managers will use a keyword search to comb through all the résumés submitted, so without these terms your résumé may never be looked at at all! Want ads for the kind of position you're pursuing (or the specific ad you're answering if there is one) will give you an idea of the words, phrases, and abbreviations you

should include. (Avoid the temptation to mention a keyword that does not relate to your background. Getting your résumé read, even getting an interview under false pretenses, won't get you the job!)

Electronic résumés are not yet used by all companies, but the advantages are making them more popular. They are inexpensive, they're fast, and they can be kept "on file" indefinitely for future reference.

Letters of Application

A *letter of application* is a *sales letter* in which you are both salesperson and product, for the purpose of an application is to *attract* an employer's attention and *persuade* her to grant you an interview. To do this, the letter presents what you can offer the employer, rather than what you want from the job.

A letter of application serves as the **cover letter** of your résumé. Like a résumé, it is a *sample of your work*; and it is, as well, an opportunity to *demonstrate*, not just talk about, your skills and personality. If it is written with flair and understanding and prepared with professional care, it is likely to hit its mark.

There are two types of application letters. A **solicited** letter is sent in response to a help-wanted ad (see, for example, Figures 9–5 and 9–8). Because such a letter will be in competition with many, perhaps several hundred, others, it must be composed with distinction. At the same time, it must refer to the ad and the specific job advertised.

An **unsolicited** letter (Figures 9–6 and 9–7) is sent to a company for which you would like to work though you know of no particular opening. The advantage of this type of application is that there will be little competition and you can define the position you would like to apply for. Too, you can send out as many of these letters as you wish, to as many companies as you are aware of; it is a good idea, though, to find out the name of a specific person to whom you can send the letter—a more effective approach than simply addressing a letter to "Personnel."

Your letter of application should *look* as good as your résumé and be prepared with the same care on plain business-size bond.

Because a letter of application must sell your qualifications, it must do more than simply restate your résumé in paragraph form. While the résumé must be factual, objective, and brief, the letter is your chance to interpret and expand. It should state explicitly how your background relates to the specific job, and it should emphasize your strongest and most pertinent characteristics. The letter should demonstrate that you know both yourself and the company.

A letter of application must communicate your ambition and enthusiasm. Yet it must, at the same time, be *modest*. It should be neither aggressive nor meek: neither pat yourself on the back nor ask for sympathy. It should *never* express dissatisfaction with a present or former job or employer. And you should avoid discussing your reasons for leaving your last job. (If asked this question at an interview, your answer, though honest, should be positive and as favorable to yourself as you can make it.)

392 Eagle Street
Terre Haute, Indiana 47807
March 1, 20–

Mr. Ikuo Saito, Vice-President
Indiana Gas and Electric Company
1114 Broad Street
Terre Haute, Indiana 47815

Dear Mr. Saito:

With several years' experience as the sole secretary of a private business, I would like to apply for the position of executive assistant that you advertised in the Terre Haute *Gazette* of Sunday, February 28, 20–.

As secretary to the Benlow Corporation here in Terre Haute, I was directly responsible to Ms. Alba Cruz, the company's owner. My services were generally those of a "gal Friday." In addition to the usual typing, filing, and bookkeeping, I was responsible for scheduling all of Ms. Cruz's appointments, screening her telephone calls and visitors, and organizing her paperwork and correspondence.

Essentially, I did everything I could to make Ms. Cruz's heavy responsibilities easier. Thus, I am familiar with the duties of an executive assistant and believe I am prepared to anticipate and meet all your expectations. I am confident, too, that, with enthusiasm and sincere effort, I can make the transition from a small business to a large corporation smoothly.

I would appreciate your giving me the opportunity to discuss my qualifications in person. I would be happy to come for an interview at your convenience, and I can be reached after 5 P.M. at 111-555-1234.

Sincerely yours,

Olga Godunov

Figure 9–5
Letter of Application I

212 Lakeview Drive
Duluth, Minnesota 34377
July 15, 2012

Dr. Jacob Larrson
Hibbing Community Health Center
73 Pine Grove Road
Hibbing, Minnesota 34380

Dear Dr. Larrson:

Last month, I completed my studies at Minnesota State University, St. Paul, to become a Physician Assistant. I have also taken the national board examination and was awarded my license in June. My faculty adviser, Professor Sara Zimmerman, suggested I apply to you for a position as your Physician Assistant.

As you will see from my enclosed résumé, I have taken courses in all the areas required of a Physician Assistant. During my residency at Downstate General Hospital, I had extensive experience interacting with patients while working closely with my supervisors to hone my diagnostic skills. The hands-on experience administering diagnostic tests as well as medications would, I am sure, be useful in your clinic setting.

My earlier experience, as a part-time office assistant to Dr. Grete Svenson, helped me develop an ability to connect with patients, to be alert to their needs and concerns. I learned that a "bedside manner" is an important in a medical office as in a hospital room.

I would like very much, Dr. Larrson, to put my skills to work for your health center. I am available for an interview Monday through Saturday during business hours. You can reach me at 111-555-1234.

Yours truly,

Arnold O'Connor

Figure 9–6
Letter of Application II

When you begin to write your letter of application, keep in mind the principles of writing sales letters:

1. *Start by attracting attention.* You must say, of course, that you are applying and mention both the specific job and how you heard about it (or, in an unsolicited letter, why you are interested in the particular company). But try to avoid a mundane opening. Instead of:

> I would like to apply for the position of legal secretary that you advertised in the *Los Angeles Times* of Sunday, August 10, 20–.

---

201 New Oak Street
Newark, New Jersey 07102
May 1, 20–

Mr. Noah Dylan
Personnel Manager
Greenwich Corporation
87-91 Partition Street
Hattiesburg, Mississippi 39411

Dear Mr. Dylan:

Gina Bassano of your Marketing Division suggested that I contact you to explore the possibility of joining your company. I am enclosing my résumé for your consideration.

Several years as Sales Supervisor at Summit & Storch have afforded me management skills that would prove highly valuable to an industry leader such as Greenwich Corporation. I am willing to relocate, and, through my experience establishing a sales office in Atlanta, I am familiar with the southern market.

I would be happy to travel to Hattiesburg for an interview. Please feel free to contact me should you have any questions about my qualifications.

Sincerely yours,

Nicolas Balaj

Figure 9–7
Letter of Application III

try something a *bit* more original:

I believe you will find that my experiences in the Alameda District
Attorney's office have prepared me well for the position of legal secretary
that you advertised in the *Los Angeles Times* of Sunday, August 10, 20—.

273 Cedar Street
Greenvale, NY 10548
January 31, 20–

Lenore Clooney, Professional Recruiter
Yonkers University Medical Center
1234 Main Street
Yonkers, NY 10707

Dear Ms. Clooney:

Having worked since 2001 in a teaching hospital with clinical resource
management programs, I would like to apply for position UH#7783a,
Director of Pharmacy, as advertised in *The New York Times* on Sunday,
January 30, 20–.

In my current position as Pharmacy Supervisor at Greenvale University
Hospital, I have had the opportunity to work with the Director of Pharmacy
in many areas beyond the specific responsibilities noted on my résumé.
I participated in staff recruitment, scheduling, and evaluation. I worked
with the Associate Hospital Director, coordinating with both the medical
and research staff. I sat in on contract negotiations with pharmaceutical
companies, and I led staff workshops in bioterrorism preparedness.

Should you grant me the chance to meet with you, I am confident that I
could demonstrate the assets and experience I would bring to your institution.

Sincerely yours,

Vita Gutierrez
(123) 555-1234
vitag@GUH.com

Figure 9–8
Letter of Application IV

2. *Continue by describing your qualifications*. Highlight your strengths and achievements and *say* how they suit you for the job at hand. Provide details and explanations (even brief anecdotes) not found on your résumé, and refer the reader to the résumé for the remaining, less pertinent facts.

3. *Assure the employer that you are the person for the job*. List verifiable facts that prove you are not exaggerating or lying. Mention the names of any familiar or prominent references you may have. In some way distinguish yourself from the mass of other qualified applicants.

4. *Conclude by requesting an interview*. Without being coercive, urge the employer to action by making it easy to contact you. Mention your e-mail address and telephone number (even though they are on your résumé) and the best hours to reach you, or state that you will call him within a few days. (Keep in mind that, while some employers will consider a follow-up call admirably ambitious, others will consider it pushy and annoying. Use your judgment.)

A complete application should contain both a letter of application and a résumé. While it is possible to write a letter so complete in detail that a résumé seems redundant, it is always most professional to include both.

It is best **not** to include copies of your letters of reference or of your school transcripts. These can be provided later if you are granted an interview. In a similar vein, do not include a photograph of yourself. The briefer the original application, the better.

A final word about salary: Basically, unless instructed by the want ad, it is best that you not broach the subject. Indeed, even if an ad requires that you mention your salary requirements, it is advisable simply to call them "negotiable." However, when you go on an interview, you should be prepared to mention a salary range (such as, $35,000–$40,000). For this reason, you should investigate both your field and, if possible, the particular company. You don't want to ask for less than you deserve or more than is reasonable.

> **Note:** An e-mailed cover letter should consist only of a brief paragraph in which you mention:
>
> 1. where you heard of the available position;
> 2. how you qualify for the position.
>
> Before sending the paragraph, cut and paste your generic text résumé into the e-mail message screen.

Follow-Up Letters

Few people nowadays send a *follow-up letter* (Figure 9–9) after an interview. For this reason alone, it can be highly effective.

A follow-up letter should be *courteous* and *brief*. It should merely thank the employer for the interview and restate your interest in the job. A reference to a successful moment at the interview is a good, personalizing touch.

212 Lakeview Drive
Duluth, Minnesota 34377
July 27, 2012

Dr. Jacob Larrson
Hibbing Community Health Center
73 Pine Grove Road
Hibbing, Minnesota 34380

Dear Dr. Larrson:

Thank you for allowing me to discuss in person my qualifications as a Physician Assistant.

Having met you and Dr. DeLoia and seen your medical center in operation, I sincerely hope I will have the chance to put my training to work for you.

Enclosed is a copy of my college transcript as well as the letters of reference you requested. I can be reached at 111-555-1234 at any time.

Sincerely yours,

Arnold O'Connor

Figure 9–9
Follow-Up Letter

Letters of Reference and Recommendation

The difference between letters of reference and recommendation is slim. A *recommendation* (Figure 9–11) is an endorsement while a *reference* (Figure 9–10) is simply a report. A recommendation is persuasive while a reference verifies facts.

Both types of letters start out the same. Each should include:

1. a statement of the letter's purpose;
2. an account of the duties performed by the applicant or of the applicant's general qualifications.

A letter of recommendation would add a third item—a concluding statement specifically *recommending* the applicant for the particular position.

Grete Svenson, MD
118 North Street, Suite 8B
Duluth, Minnesota 34377

July 26, 2012

Dr. Jacob Larrson
Hibbing Community Health Center
73 Pine Grove Road
Hibbing, Minnesota 34380

Dear Dr. Larrson:

I am happy to provide the information you requested regarding Arnold O'Connor, with the understanding that this information will be kept confidential.

Mr. O'Connor was a part-time office assistant for my private practice during his senior year in high school, from July 2007 until August 2008. He was a dependable employee and never late despite his need to balance school and work. He performed his duties accurately and conscientiously, and he got on well with both his coworkers and my patients. I considered him a hardworking, trustworthy, employee.

Sincerely yours,

Grete Svenson, MD

Figure 9–10
Letter of Reference

PHYSICIAN ASSISTANT PROGRAM
DECKER HALL, ROOM 19
MINNESOTA STATE UNIVERSITY
ST. PAUL, MINNESOTA 34333

July 26, 2012

Dr. Jacob Larrson
Hibbing Community Health Center
73 Pine Grove Road
Hibbing, Minnesota 34380

Dear Dr. Larrson:

Arnold O'Connor was a student in three of my courses during
his studies to become a Physician Assistant. He was always an
outstanding student.

Mr. O'Connor demonstrated his thorough grasp of the subject
matter in his class performance as well as in lab and fieldwork.
His assignments were always executed with conscientiousness
and punctuality. Moreover, he was an enthusiastic participant in
class discussions and helped make the courses more rewarding
experiences for everyone.

Therefore, I can recommend Mr. O'Connor, without hesitation, for
the position of Physician Assistant at your health center.

Truly yours,

Sara Zimmerman
Associate Professor

Figure 9–11
Letter of Recommendation

Note: Before you write a reference or recommendation, be
sure your company has no policy forbidding them (to avoid
possible lawsuits or complaints). If you do write such a letter,
it is advisable to mark both the envelope and letter "Confidential" to protect yourself and the applicant.

Declining a Job Offer

A fortunate job applicant may find himself or herself in the position of choosing from several job offers. Or a job may be offered that does not meet the applicant's needs or expectations. In such situations, a courteous, discreet letter declining the job (Figure 9–12) will preserve a potentially valuable business contact and leave open the possibility of future employment.

212 Lakeview Drive
Duluth, Minnesota 34377
August 1, 2012

Dr. Dirko Goncic
Cloquet Family Medical Center
322 River Road
Cloquet, Minnesota 34379

Dear Dr. Goncic:

Thank you for taking time to discuss with me both my career goals and the needs of your medical practice. I appreciate your offering me a position as office manager.

Unfortunately, I must decline your offer at this time. As I mentioned when we met, I am eager to put my newly acquired medical skills to use and would like to begin working as a Physician Assistant.

I am, nevertheless, disappointed that we will not be working together. I hope you will understand my decision.

Yours truly,

Arnold O'Connor

Figure 9–12
Letter Declining a Job Offer

Rejecting a Job Applicant

Every employer must face the unpleasant task of rejecting job applicants. When the search for a new employee has been properly conducted, the successful candidate will be greatly outnumbered by the unsuccessful candidates. While a personal letter explaining specific reasons for an applicant's rejection is professional and preferable, a form letter (Figure 9–13) is more often used as a way to reject in general terms all the unsuccessful candidates.

Per Linqvist, MD
118 North Street, Suite 6C
Duluth, Minnesota 34377

July 2, 20—

Dear

    I am sorry to inform you that I have filled the position of Physician Assistant for which you recently applied.

    Please be assured that your qualifications were thoroughly reviewed, and only after careful consideration did I offer the position to the candidate whose experience and career goals were most compatible with the nature of my medical practice.

    Thank you for your interest and time. I wish you success in your career.

    Yours truly,

Per Linqvist, MD

Figure 9–13
Applicant Rejection Letter

Letters of Resignation

Landing a new job usually means resigning an old one. Speaking personally to your old employer is appropriate, but putting the resignation in writing is also advisable.

Like refusals, resignations (Figure 9–14) must convey a negative message as positively as possible. Even when you may be delighted to be leaving or feel hostile toward your old boss, your letter of resignation should express regrets but not anger. Be sure to:

1. State that the letter is your resignation, mentioning the date on which you would like to leave.
2. Express appreciation for your old job and/or regret at leaving.
3. Offer assistance with any work that you will be leaving undone or with helping the person who will replace you.

201 New Oak Street
Newark, New Jersey 07102
June 12, 20—

Mr. Seamus O'Toole
President
Summit & Storch
875 Davidson Street
Newark, New Jersey 07554

Dear Mr. O'Toole:

My eight years at Summit & Storch have been rewarding, so it is with regret that I must submit my resignation, effective June 26, 20—.

A management opportunity has arisen, and I feel I must pursue it. Still, I shall always appreciate the support and encouragement you have shown me.

I am prepared to remain at my duties for the next two weeks to ease the transition for my successor. Please let me know if this is acceptable.

Sincerely yours,

Nicolas Balaj

Figure 9–14
Letter of Resignation

LETTERS OF INTRODUCTION   119

You may mention a reason for leaving (such as an opportunity for advancement), but this is optional.

Remember, leaving a job on good terms is in your best interest. Even if you plan never to return, you may need references in a future job search. (It is even possible that your supervisor may also leave the company and you could find yourselves working together again someday!) So keep the resignation letter civil and brief.

Letters of Introduction

Rather different from but not entirely unrelated to employment letters are *letters of introduction* (Figure 9–15). These are written to a business associate on behalf of a third person (such as an employee, customer,

---

Jacob Larrson, MD
Hibbing Community Health Center
73 Pine Grove Road
Hibbing, Minnesota 34380

June 20, 2013

Dr. Tatsuo Miura
Midwest Medical Association
1232 Twelfth Avenue
Madison, Wisconsin 57555

Dear Tatsuo:

Arnold O'Connor has been my Physician Assistant for the past year and will be attending the Annual Midwest Medical Conference in my stead.

Since this will be his first experience at a conference, I would greatly appreciate your taking him under your wing. Introducing him to others in attendance would be very helpful. Also, please steer him toward lectures, in addition to your own, from which he might benefit.

I am sorry we won't be seeing each other at the conference, and I especially regret missing your lecture. However, I will be in Madison next month and insist that you allow me to take you to dinner at that time.

With much appreciation,

Jacob Larrson

Figure 9–15
Letter of Introduction

or client). Such a letter is written when one person you know would like to establish a business relationship with another person whom you also know but whom he himself does not.

The letter of introduction you write in such a situation should include three points:

1. the relationship between you and the person being "introduced";
2. your reason for introducing him to your reader;
3. what you (or he) would like the reader to do for him.

The letter of introduction is sort of a cross between a request and a reference. It should be worded with *courtesy*.

Generally, the letter of introduction is given to the individual being introduced, who in turn delivers it in person. However, it is customary to forward a copy of the letter, along with an explanatory (and less formal) cover letter, so that your reader will anticipate the visit.

■■■■■■ PRACTICE CORRESPONDENCE

Prepare your own employment correspondence according to the following instructions.

A. List all the facts that you can think of about your personality, background, and experiences. Then arrange the list in a logical order and decide on categories under which to group the facts. From this worksheet, prepare your résumé.

B. Imagine the ideal job for which you would like to apply. With this job in mind, write an unsolicited letter of application to a prospective employer and ask for an interview.

C. Now imagine that you have been offered your ideal job. Write a letter of resignation to your current employer.

10.
In-House Correspondence

The letters discussed so far were, for the most part, intended to be sent to people outside one's own company. As messages to customers, clients, and other business associates, they placed heavy emphasis on business promotion and goodwill. But business people frequently must communicate in writing with employees of their own company. The primary purpose of *in-house correspondence* is to share information.

The Interoffice Memorandum

While the use of personal computers and e-mail have reduced the need, within an organization, to communicate on paper, the need does still exist. Communication may begin on the computer screen or telephone, or even face-to-face, but "putting it in writing" for the record is often a wise precaution against future misunderstanding. The format for this written record is known as an interoffice memorandum.

Memorandums, more usually called *memos*, are the form commonly used for *short*, relatively *informal* messages between members of the same organization (see Figures 10–1 and 10–2). The memo provides a simplified, standardized format for communicating information *concisely*. The many uses of memos include announcements and instructions, statements of policy, and informal reports.

Because memos are usually used between people who have a regular working relationship, the *tone* of memos tends to be more informal than the tone of other business letters. Company jargon, for example, is permissible in a memo. Similarly, the writer can usually assume that the reader knows the basic facts and so can get to the heart of the message with little buildup. Note, however, that the level of formality should reflect the relationship between the writer and the reader.

At the same time, a memo, like any piece of written communication, must be prepared with care. It must be **printed** neatly and contain **complete**, **accurate** information. It should adhere to the principles of standard English and maintain a **courteous** tone no matter how familiar the correspondents may be.

Unlike other types of business letters, the memo is **not** prepared on company letterhead. Nor does it include an inside address, salutation, or complimentary closing. A memo is a streamlined form, and, indeed, many companies provide a preestablished template to speed up memo preparation even further.

C.P. Dalloway & Sons
Interoffice Memo

TO: Charles Dalloway, Jr.
FROM: Clarissa Woolf
DATE: August 18, 20–
SUBJECT: Search for a New Warehouse Manager

Here is the progress report you requested about our search for a new
warehouse manager.

We have now interviewed eight individuals and narrowed our choices
to three:

1. David Siu—has worked in our Diego Street warehouse for six years, frequently assisting and filling in for the retiring manager, Fernando Sanchez.

2. Changdi Ramdas—has been with Dalloway for four years and is temporary
   warehouse manager on Andrews Street, while Ernst Freund is on
   sick leave.

3. Sean Williams—is currently a warehouse manager for Equicom; his three
   years there have earned him excellent references.

I will be meeting with Angela Petroni and Jim Singleton tomorrow, August
19, at 9:30 A.M., to discuss the candidates and make a decision. Your
presence at the meeting (in Ms. Petroni's office) is, of course, welcome.

CW

Figure 10–1
Interoffice Memorandum I

Goleta Motors, Inc.   Memo

TO: All Sales Representatives

FROM: Peter Koulikourdis

DATE: April 27, 20—

SUBJECT: Rescheduling of Monthly Sales Meeting

The May Monthly Sales Meeting has been rescheduled. Instead of Tuesday, May 3, we will meet on

Wednesday, May 4, at 10:30 A.M.

in the Conference Room. Please mark your calendar accordingly.

PK

Figure 10–2
Interoffice Memorandum II

Whether or not a prescribed format is available, most memos use a standard heading: the company name about one inch from the top followed by the term "Interoffice Memo." Beneath this, four basic subheadings are used:

TO:
FROM:
DATE:
SUBJECT:

(Some companies also include space for such details as office numbers, e-mail addresses, or telephone extensions.)

The TO: line indicates the name of the person to whom the memo is sent. Courtesy titles (such as *Mr.* and *Ms.*) are generally used only to show respect to a superior; job titles, departments, and room numbers may be included to avoid confusion. When several people will be receiving copies, a CC notation may be added or an inclusive term used (such as "TO: All Personnel").

The FROM: line indicates the name of the person sending the memo. No courtesy title should be used, but a job title, department, e-mail address, or extension number may be included for clarity or convenience.

The DATE: line indicates in standard form the date on which the memo is sent.

The SUBJECT: line serves as a title and so should briefly but thoroughly describe the content of the memo.

The body of the memo begins three to four lines below the subject line. Like any piece of writing, it should be logically organized. But it should also be **concise**: the information should be immediately accessible to the reader. For this reason, data are often itemized and paragraphs are numbered. Statistics should be presented in tables.

The body of most memos can be divided into three general sections:

An *introduction* states the main idea or purpose.
A *detailed discussion* presents the actual information being conveyed.
A *conclusion* may make recommendations or call for further actions.

> **Note:** Memos are not usually signed. The writer's initials appear below the message, and if she chooses she may sign her initials over the printed ones or at the FROM line. Reference initials and enclosure notation are placed below the writer's initials along the left margin.

Minutes

Within most organizations, meetings among members of departments or committees are a regular occurrence. Some meetings are held at fixed intervals (such as weekly or monthly), and others are called for special reasons. *Minutes* (Figure 10–3) are a written record of everything that transpires at a meeting. They are prepared for the company files, for the reference of those in attendance, and for the information of absentees.

Minutes are prepared by a secretary who takes thorough notes during the proceedings. Afterward, he prepares a *draft* and includes all the pertinent information. (It is usually the secretary's responsibility to decide which statements or actions at a meeting are insignificant and so should be omitted from the minutes.)

In preparing the minutes, the secretary may include complete versions of statements and papers read at the meeting. (Copies are provided by the member involved.) The minutes of *formal* meetings (of, for example, large corporations or government agencies), where legal considerations are involved, are made *verbatim*, that is, they include, word for word, everything that is said or done.

The format used for minutes varies from one organization to another. But the minutes of any meeting should contain certain basic facts:

1. the name of the organization;
2. the place, date, and time of the meeting;
3. whether the meeting is regular (monthly, special, etc.);
4. the name of the person presiding;
5. a record of attendance (for small meetings, a list of those present or absent; for large meetings, the number of members in attendance);
6. a reference to the minutes of the previous meeting (a statement that they were read and either accepted or revised, or that the reading was dispensed with);
7. an account of all reports, motions, or resolutions made (including all necessary details and the results of votes taken);
8. the date, time, and place of the next meeting;
9. the time of adjournment.

Formal minutes would include, in addition to greater detail, the names of all those who make and second motions and resolutions, and the voting record of each person present. The secretary's name (and signature) appear at the end of the minutes beneath the formal complimentary closing, "Respectfully submitted."

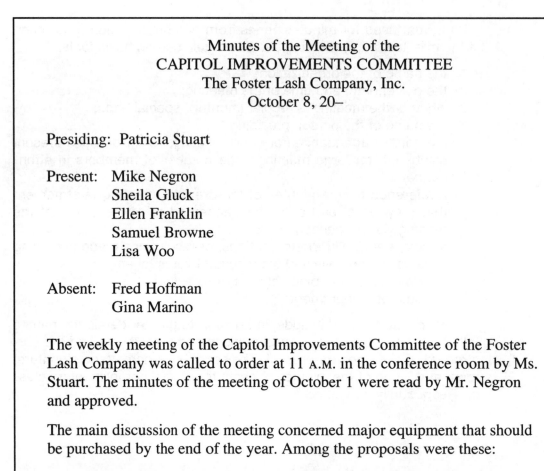

Minutes of the Meeting of the
CAPITOL IMPROVEMENTS COMMITTEE
The Foster Lash Company, Inc.
October 8, 20–

Presiding: Patricia Stuart

Present: Mike Negron
           Sheila Gluck
           Ellen Franklin
           Samuel Browne
           Lisa Woo

Absent: Fred Hoffman
           Gina Marino

The weekly meeting of the Capitol Improvements Committee of the Foster Lash Company was called to order at 11 A.M. in the conference room by Ms. Stuart. The minutes of the meeting of October 1 were read by Mr. Negron and approved.

The main discussion of the meeting concerned major equipment that should be purchased by the end of the year. Among the proposals were these:

Ms. Woo presented information regarding three varieties of office copying machines. On the basis of her cost analysis and relative performance statistics, it was decided, by majority vote, to recommend the purchase of a CBM X-12 copier.

Mr. Browne presented a request from the clerical staff for new personal digital assistants. Several employees have complained about the limited memory of their older units, as well as a compatibility problem with newer PCs. Ms. Franklin and Mr. Browne are to further investigate the need for new PDAs and prepare a cost comparison of available brands and models.

The committee will discuss the advisability of upgrading account executives' laptop computers to tablets. The report will be presented by Sheila Gluck at the next meeting, to be held on October 15, 20–, at 11 A.M. in the conference room.

The meeting adjourned at 11:45 A.M.

Respectfully submitted,

Ellen Franklin, Secretary

Figure 10–3
Minutes

███ **PRACTICE CORRESPONDENCE**

Prepare the in-house correspondence called for in each of the following situations.

A. Your employer, Penelope Louden, requested a schedule of the data processors' planned vacations so that she may decide whether or not to arrange for temporary help during the summer months. The schedule is as follows: Josie Thompkins, July 1–15; Calvin Bell, July 15–29; Stephen James, July 22–August 5; Jennifer Coles, August 12–26. Prepare a memo to Ms. Louden informing her of the schedule and observing that at least three processors will always be present— except during the week of July 22, when both Mr. Bell and Mr. James will be on vacation. Ask if she'd like you to arrange for a temporary processor for that week.

B. As administrative assistant to the president of Conway Products, Inc., it is your responsibility to make reservations at a local restaurant for the annual Christmas party. Because of the high cost per person, you would like to have as accurate a guest list as possible. Write a memo to all the employees requesting that they let you know by December 1 whether they plan to attend.

C. As secretary to the Labor Grievances Committee of the Slate and Johnson Luggage Company, you must prepare the minutes of the monthly meeting held on September 23. At the meeting, you took the following notes:

1. Called to order 4 P.M., employees' cafeteria, by Mr. Falk.
2. Presiding: Mr. Falk; Present: Mr. Baum, Ms. Dulugatz, Mr. Fenster, Ms. Garcia, Ms. Penn; Absent: Mr. Sun.
3. Correction made in minutes of previous meeting (August 21): Ms. Dulugatz, not Ms. Penn, to conduct study of employee washroom in warehouse. Approved as corrected.
4. Mr. Fenster presented results of survey of office employees. Most frequent complaints agreed on. Fenster to arrange to present these complaints to Board of Directors.
5. Report on condition of warehouse employee washrooms presented by Ms. Dulugatz. Accepted with editorial revision.
6. Adjourned 5:15 P.M. Next meeting at same time and place on October 22.

D. As secretary to the Highridge Tenants Association, prepare minutes from the following notes taken at the emergency meeting on May 4, 20—.

1. Called to order 7:30 P.M., lobby, by Ms. Gingold.
2. 102 members present, 13 absent, all officers present.
3. Reading of minutes of last meeting dispensed with.

4. Officers' Reports—
Vice-President read through "red herring" sent by landlord to tenants. Explained more difficult clauses. Explained lengthy court procedure before actual cooperative offering can be made.
Treasurer reported balance of $487.10. Observed need for minimum of $3000 to retain attorney to negotiate with landlord. Requested members with unpaid dues to see him after meeting.
5. Motions—
The President called for committee to search for a lawyer to represent tenants. Motion made and carried that floor captains will constitute the committee headed by the President.
Motion to meet again to vote on search committee's selection made and carried.
6. Adjourned 9:30 P.M.

11.
News Releases

A *news release* (Figures 11–1 and 11–2) is a form of publicity writing. It is usually an announcement of an event or development within a company. Such occurrences as meetings, appointments, promotions, and expansions, as well as the introduction of new products or services and the dissemination of financial information, are all potential subjects for news releases.

News releases are sent to company and industry publications and the mass media (specifically newspapers, radio, and television) in the hope that the editor will approve the release for publication or broadcast. In order to be accepted by an editor, therefore, a release must do more than promote a company's image and goodwill; it must be **newsworthy** and **timely**; that is, it must interest the audience.

Like memos and minutes, news releases do not use standard business letter format. Nor do they use the "*you*-oriented" tone of voice referred to so often in this book. Both the layout and language of a news release are aimed at making it "copy ready." The less rewriting a release requires, the more likely an editor will be to accept it.

A news release should be *concise* and *straightforward;* it should contain no superfluous words. Nor should it contain confusing words: its meaning should be easily understood. Moreover, it should be written in an impersonal style. Your company, for example, should be referred to by name, not as "our company" or "we." Individuals, including yourself, should similarly be referred to by name—almost as if an outsider or reporter had written the story. References to dates and times, as well, should be specific. (Words like *today, tomorrow,* and *yesterday* are pointless when you can't be sure when your release will see print.)

The first, or lead paragraph of a news release is the most important. Since an editor, if space is needed for a more newsworthy item, may chop away parts of your release from the bottom up, the lead paragraph should be capable of standing on its own. It should summarize the event and contain all the essential details. Following paragraphs should elaborate with additional information in order of importance. As in all business writing, **accuracy** and **completeness** of details are essential; but in a news release even a spelling error could cause an editor to doubt your reliability and reject your story.

A news release may be prepared on either letterhead or plain paper. Ideally it should be limited to one page. If you must, however, use more than one sheet, the word "MORE" should appear in the lower right corner of every page but the last, and all pages should be numbered successively in the upper right corner. The end of the release should be indicated with one of the following symbols:

-xxx-
000
# # #
-30-

The heading for a news release must include a release date:

FOR RELEASE
February 2, 20—

FOR RELEASE AFTER
4 P.M., February 1, 20—

FOR IMMEDIATE RELEASE

Across from the release date, flush right, indicate (in numerical form) the date on which the news release was prepared.

Also in the heading, if letterhead is not used, should be the company name and address as well as the telephone and fax numbers and e-mail addresses of people whom an editor could contact for additional information. Following the heading you may either include a tentative title or leave an inch of white space for an editor to insert a title of her own.

The body of the news release should be double spaced; paragraphs should be indented five spaces. Margins of at least one inch should be left all around for copyeditors' comments. If photographs are enclosed with the release, they should be clearly labeled with a description of the event and the names of any people depicted.

Finally, the release should be addressed to The Editor, if sent to a newspaper, or to The News Director, if sent to a radio or television station. Of course, use the person's name if you know it. The envelope should bear the words: "NEWS RELEASE ENCLOSED."

NEWS RELEASE

Ericson Electronics, Inc.
1111 Maitland Plaza
Tremont, Massachusetts 52131
(800) 555-1234
eei.com

April Frank
Editor-in-Chief
Audio-Video Dealer Monthly
(111) 123-4567

FOR IMMEDIATE RELEASE   7/7/—

SALES, NET UP AT ERICSON

Tremont, July 7, 20—. Ericson Electronics announced significantly higher second-quarter earnings despite slightly lower revenues. A spokesperson for Ericson credited a combination of improved sales mix and operating efficiencies in North America as well as a generally stronger overseas performance for the improvement.

For the three months, the TV and radio manufacturer had a net of $56 million, up 21.7% from last year's $46 million while revenue of $2.81 million declined 1.3%.

Ericson said its unit shipments in North America were down, but less than the industry's overall 3% decline, and a combination of product mix, manufacturing efficiencies, and more favorable material costs resulted in improved margins. The company expects that, along with the industry, its total shipments will be down from last year's record because of the currently high level of TV inventories at retail.

"Overall, we're pleased with the quarter and with the progress it represents toward our full-year goals," said chairman Kwow Joong. "Our North and Latin American divisions again put up outstanding numbers, and our European and Asian results met our expectations. We look forward to significant operating improvement through this year."

-30-

Figure 11–1
News Release I

NEWS RELEASE

National Organization of Retired Persons
Fort Worth, Texas 76111
Zenaida Plonov, Publicity Director
(800) 555-1234   *zplonov@NORP.org*

Alicia Hidalgo
The Editor
Fort Worth Gazette
(111) 123-4567

FOR RELEASE AFTER
3 P.M., April 7, 20—   4/4/—

ALVIN BANKS NAMED RETIRED PERSON OF THE YEAR

Fort Worth, April 7, 20—. Alvin Banks, outgoing president of the Fort Worth Chapter of the National Organization of Retired Persons, was named "Retired Person of the Year" at a luncheon in his honor on April 7.

During his two years in office, Mr. Banks, the retired owner and manager of Banks Building and Supply Company, helped the Fort Worth Chapter grow from 53 members to its present high of 175 members. He instituted a number of the organization's current programs, including a part-time job placement service and a guest lecture series.

Mr. Banks will be succeeded as president by Mrs. Beatrice Toller, a retired buyer for Grayson's Department Store.

The Fort Worth Chapter of the National Organization of Retired Persons meets Wednesday evenings at 7 P.M. at the Presbyterian Church on Humboldt Street. Meetings are open to the public and all retired persons are welcome to join.

# # #

Figure 11–2
News Release II

▄▄▄▄ PRACTICE CORRESPONDENCE

For each of the following situations, prepare a publicity-minded news release.

A. As director of the accounting department of the Waterford Stores, send a news release to the company newsletter announcing the addition of a new member to your staff. Marlon Strong, a certified public accountant, earned his bachelor's degree at Brockton College, where he was president of the Young Accountants Club during his junior and senior years. Before coming to Waterford, he was a junior accountant with Moyer and Moyer, a private accounting firm. Quote yourself as praising Mr. Strong's background and expertise and welcoming him to the company.

B. On Saturday, July 31, at 11 A.M., the Paperback Power Bookstore at 7777 Main Street, Little Falls, New Jersey, will host an autograph session for Lillian Lockhart, author of the current bestseller, *The Office Worker's Weekday Diet Book*. The book, published by Knoll Books at $23.95, was described in *The New York Times* as "a valuable, must-read book for anyone who works in an office." Ms. Lockhart, a registered nutritionist, is also author of *Eat and Run: A Diet for Joggers*, among other books. Emil Lazar, owner of Paperback Power, has said that Ms. Lockhart's appearance at the store will be the first of a series of autographing events at the bookstore. Prepare a news release for the *Little Falls Press* announcing the event.

C. The Reliable Drug Store, 120 Franklin Street, Roscoe, New York, has been serving the community for over twenty years. On Monday, May 3, will be the grand opening of a Health Food Annex to be located in what used to be Fred's Barber Shop, just to the right of Reliable's main store, at 118 Franklin Street. According to Marjorie Mansfield, present owner and daughter of the founder of Reliable Drug, Hiram Mansfield, the expansion was prompted by widespread interest in health foods as well as by increasing demand for top-quality vitamins and minerals. Ms. Mansfield said, "We intend to offer to small-town residents the variety of a big-city health-food store and plan to carry everything from powdered yeast and protein to frozen yogurt and dried fruit." Write a news release to be sent to the local radio station making the expansion sound as newsworthy as possible.

12.
Business Reports and Proposals

Reports

Information plays a vital role in the business world, nowadays more than ever before. The latest advances in computers, information-processing systems, and telecommunications have in fact made information a commodity in itself and those who process information valued members of the business community.

The purpose of a *business report* is to convey essential information in an organized, useful format. And despite technological advances, the ability to accumulate data, organize facts, and compose a readable text remains a highly marketable skill.

A well-prepared business report will provide **complete**, **accurate** information about an aspect of a company's operations. The subject of a report may vary from expenses to profits, products to sales, marketing trends to customer relations. The information provided by a report is often meant to influence decisions, to be used in determining changes, improvements, or solutions to problems. Therefore, the report must also be **clear**, **concise**, and **readable**.

The *format* of a business report may vary, from a brief *informal report* intended for in-house use to a voluminous *formal report* intended for national public distribution. Some reports consist entirely of text, while others consist of statistics; still other reports may employ a combination of prose, tables, charts, and graphs.

The frequency of reports also varies. Some are unique, submitted one time only as a result of a special project or circumstance. Others are recurring, submitted routinely (weekly, monthly, quarterly, etc.), often on a preprinted form or in a preestablished format.

The *style* of a report depends upon the audience. An informal report (Figures 12–1, 12–2, and 12–3) to be read only by close associates may be worded personally; in such a report "I" or "we" is acceptable. A formal report, on the other hand, must be impersonal and expressed entirely in the third person. Note the difference:

Informal: I recommend that the spring campaign concentrate on Internet and television advertising.

Formal: It is recommended that the spring campaign concentrate on Internet and television advertising.

Informal: After discussing the matter with our department managers, we came up with the following information.

Formal: The following report is based upon information provided by the managers of the Accounting, Marketing, Personnel, and Advertising Departments.

Whether formal or informal, however, the wording of a report should be **simple** and **direct**.

The *type* of report may vary, according to how the facts are presented and whether the facts are interpreted.

1. **A Record Report** merely states facts, describing the status of a company or a division of a company at a particular point in time.
2. **A Progress Report** also states facts, tracing developments that have occurred over a period of time.
3. **A Statistical Report** presents numerical data, usually in the form of charts, tables, and graphs.
4. **An Investigative Report** is based on a study or investigation of a particular situation or issue. Such a report presents the newly accumulated data; it may also analyze the data.
5. **A Recommendation Report** is an investigative report taken one step further, providing specific recommendations based on the information provided.

There are three important *rules* to keep in mind when preparing any business report:

1. Cite your sources. *Always* let your reader know where your information comes from so that it may be verified.
2. Date your report. Business is volatile; facts and situations change daily, if not hourly. Your information could become outdated very quickly.
3. *Always* keep a copy of your report for your own reference.

Informal Reports

The informal report is the most common form of business report. It is usually short, five pages or fewer, and is generally drafted in the form of a memo (Figure 12–1) or a variation of a memo. Sometimes, if sent to someone outside the company, the informal report may be written as a letter (Figure 12–2).

The tone and style of an informal report will vary according to the subject and audience. But whether friendly or impersonal, a report must always be worded with courtesy and tact.

An informal report must often be prepared quickly, requiring that information be gathered more casually and unscientifically than for a formal report. Nevertheless, no matter how minor the topic nor how short the time, any business report must be **thorough** and **factual**.

The best approach to accumulating data is to begin by defining your *purpose*. If you can express precisely the reason for your report, you will know what information to look for.

Once your data are assembled, the second phase of report writing is *organization*. You must arrange your facts in a logical sequence that can be easily followed.

Finally, the nature of your data and your system of organization will determine your form of *presentation*. If your report calls for prose, organize your paragraphs:

First Paragraph: Present the main idea clearly and concisely.

Middle Paragraphs: Develop the main point with supporting details and information.

Final Paragraph: State your *objective* conclusion. If called for, your own comments and recommendations may be included at the end.

TO: Mr. Marvin Dawson

FROM: Junzo Roshi

DATE: February 7, 20—

SUBJECT: Report on Secretarial Staff Overtime for January

As you requested, I have computed the number of overtime hours worked by the secretaries of the various departments and the cost of that overtime to the company.

Department	Employee	Hourly Wage	Number of Occasions	Total Hours	Total Cost @ Time and a Half
Executive	Ann Rogers	$15.00	6	15	$337.50
	Wilma Toynbee	15.00	5	14	315.00
Marketing	Maribel Cruz	10.00	8	17	255.00
Accounting	Nicole Foire	10.00	8	18	270.00
Personnel	Judy Hecht	10.00	10	21	315.00
	TOTALS		37	85	$1492.50

The cost of hiring a clerical assistant for 35 hours a week at $7.00 an hour would be $245.00, or $980.00 and 140 hours a month. This would save the company approximately $512.50 yet provide an additional 55 clerical hours.

JC

Figure 12–1
Informal Report (Memo)

Note: In a short, informal report, it is often a good idea to *itemize* your data. This may simply mean numbering your paragraphs, or it may mean arranging tables of statistics. However you do it, itemization makes a report seem more organized and easier to read.

International Industries, Inc.
3000 Avenue of the Americas
New York, NY 10019

Dear Shareholder:

Subject: Third-Quarter Report

Third-quarter earnings continued at record levels due to a significant increase in International's petroleum operations. Earnings for the first nine months exceeded last year's full-year results.

International Industries' third-quarter income from continuing operations was $42,351,000 or $1.25 per common share, a 40% increase over the income of $30,330,000 or 89 cents per common share for the same period last year.

Operating income for International's petroleum operations increased 53% over the third quarter of last year, contributing over 79% of International's income.

As a result of depressed conditions in the automotive and railroad markets, International's earnings from fabricated metal products continued to decline. International Chemicals' overall quarterly earnings declined, although full-year income from International Chemicals should be substantially above last year's levels.

International Industries is a leading manufacturer of petroleum equipment and services, metal products, and chemicals, with annual sales of $2 billion.

Laura M. Carson
Chairperson and Chief Executive Officer

Wayne G. Wagner
President and Chief Operating Officer

November 10, 2011

Figure 12–2 (Continued on page 139)
Informal Report (Letter)

2

INTERNATIONAL INDUSTRIES, INC.
Consolidated Statement of Income (Unaudited)
(In thousands, except per share)

| | For the three months ended September 30 | |
	2005	2006
Revenues:		
Net Sales	$517,858	$454,866
Income from investments in other companies	8,729	4,046
Other income (loss), net	2,599	990
Total revenues	$529,186	$459,902
Costs and expenses:		
Cost of goods sold	$339,851	$303,893
Selling, general & administrative	111,384	91,597
Interest	9,456	13,001
Minority interest	1,600	705
Total costs and expenses	$462,291	$409,196
Income before items shown below	$66,895	$50,706
Taxes on income	24,544	20,376
Income from continuing operations	$42,351	$30,330
Income from discontinued operations, net of income taxes	—	2,346
Income before cumulative effect of accounting change	$42,351	$32,676
Cumulative effect of accounting change	—	—
Net income	$42,351	$32,676
Income per share of common stock (*):		
Income from continuing operations	$1.25	$.89
Net income per share	$1.25	$.96

NOTE: (*) Income per share of common stock has been calculated
after deduction for preferred stock dividend requirements
of $.03 per share of common stock for the three months
ended September 30.

Figure 12–2 (Continued)
Informal Report (Letter)

TRAVEL EXPENSE REPORT

NAME: _____

DEPARTMENT: _____

DATE: _____

DESTINATION: _____

DATES OF TRAVEL: _____

PURPOSE OF TRIP: _____

_____

_____

TRANSPORTATION: _____ $

HOTEL: _____ $

CAR RENTAL: _____ $

MEALS: _____ $

OTHER (itemize): _____ $

_____ $

_____ $

TOTAL: $

(For proper reimbursement be sure to attach all receipts.)

Figure 12–3
Informal Report (Preprinted Form)

Formal Reports

A formal report (Figures 12–4 through 12–11) is not only longer but also more thorough than an informal report. It requires more extensive information gathering and is presented in a more stylized format. It is always presented objectively and relies on extensive details for documentation.

As for informal reports, begin preparing your formal report by pinpointing your topic. State the problem to be solved as precisely as you can. Then decide what information is needed to solve that problem and the techniques required to gather that information. Typical methods of information gathering include library research, surveys and interviews, and experimentation.

When your investigation is complete and you have collected your data, you must organize and analyze the facts. Your interpretation may or may not be included in the final version of the report, but your own understanding and grasp of the material is essential before you begin to write.

When finished, your formal report will consist of the following parts:

1. TITLE PAGE: This page will include the title of the report as well as the name of the person who prepared the report, the name of the person for whom it was prepared, and the date on which it was completed. The title page, therefore, will contain a great deal of white space.
2. TABLE OF CONTENTS: This page will be outlined in advance, but it must be prepared last. It consists of a list of all the headings and subheadings in the report and the number of the page on which each section begins.
3. INTRODUCTION: Unlike the introduction to a college term paper, this section is *not* an opening statement leading into your main topic. Rather, it is a statement of three specific facts:
   a. The purpose of your report (what the report demonstrates or proves);
   b. The scope of your report (what the report does and does *not* include);
   c. The method by which you gathered your information.
4. SUMMARY: This section is a concise statement of the main points covered in the report. Think of it as a courtesy for the busy executive who will not have enough time to read your entire report.
5. BODY: This is the essence of your report. It is the organized presentation of the data you have accumulated.
6. CONCLUSION: This is an *objective* statement of what the report has shown.
7. RECOMMENDATIONS: These should be made, when called for, on *the basis of the facts* included in the report. They should flow logically from the objective conclusion.
8. APPENDIX: This section consists of supplementary information, often in the form of graphs and charts, that does not fit into the body of the report but that is essential to substantiate the data.
9. BIBLIOGRAPHY: A listing of references used in preparing the report is required whenever printed material or web sites have been consulted. Entries are listed alphabetically by author's last name.

Web sites are also listed alphabetically. Proper format varies from field to field, so you should consult a manual or style sheet. The following examples, though, will serve as general models:

Book: Criscito, Pat. *How to Write Better Résumés and Cover Letters.* Hauppauge: Barron's, 2003.
Periodical: Rowland, Mary. "Sorting Through the Tax Changes." *The New York Times*, November 4, 2003, section 3, page 17.
Web site: www.usbusinessmonthly.com/offshoredrilling

An Examination of Company Preparedness
in the Event of a
Bioterrorism Attack

Prepared by   Rachel Orloff
                   Assistant Security Manager

Prepared for   Winston Chin
                   President, TechnoChem Corp.

February 22, 20–

Figure 12–4
Formal Report—Title Page

2

TABLE OF CONTENTS

Figure 12–5
Formal Report—Table of Contents

3

INTRODUCTION

The purpose of this report is to examine the preparedness level of each division of the TechnoChem Corporation in the event of a bioterrorism attack occurring on either company premises or in the immediately surrounding community.

This report does not consider more conventional security concerns such as burglary response, or safety considerations such as fire evacuation plans, nor does it consider the possibility of a cyber attack.

The information for this report was gathered from the following sources:

- U.S. Department of Homeland Security advisories and press releases

- U.S. Department of Health and Human Services bulletins

- Transcripts of testimony by the Directors of the FBI and CIA before the Senate Select Committee on Intelligence

- Published recommendations of several noted experts in the field of bioterrorism preparedness

- Interviews with local first response teams (police, fire, medical, and so on)

- Interviews with division managers and personnel

- Inspection of the physical facility in the company of division managers

- Company records, especially personnel files

Figure 12–6
Formal Report—Introduction

4

SUMMARY

This report demonstrates that TechnoChem Corporation, while not a "high-profile target," is a potential "soft target" for a small-scale biological, chemical, or radiological attack by either a recognized terrorist cell or an unanticipated "civilian" sympathizer.

The report outlines the minimum preparedness requirements as indicated by several noted experts. These include a two-pronged approach:

I. Deterrence

    A. Personnel—pre-hire background checks and post-hire follow-up security checks

    B. Physical Plant—monitoring of all people with access; screening of all materials brought in; securing of ventilation system

II. Survival

    A. Response to an attack—response plans; survival supplies; alternative communications systems

    B. Recovery from an attack—alternative work sites; cleanup requirements

This report then examines each division of TechnoChem Corporation with respect to the indicated preparedness requirements.

Figure 12–7
Formal Report—Summary

The most difficult part of a report to prepare, of course, is the body. Since this is where the bulk of your work will be focused, you should proceed systematically:

1. *Research*—Your report will consist of information, and you must determine where to find it. Sources may include your own experience, company files, the Internet and other computer-based data sources, people (by means of interviews and questionnaires), industry and government publications, and other printed literature (such as books and articles).
2. *Organization*—When you have gathered the necessary data, you must arrange it logically. The system you use will be determined by your topic. Some reports require a chronological presentation. In other reports, the purpose will suggest division into categories: Are you comparing, ranking, examining cause and effect? Whatever arrangement you decide on should be emphasized with subtitles and headings.

11

Survival Supplies

Robert Wolfson[1] recommends these items for each work site:

1. Duct tape and plastic sheeting sufficient to make the site airtight.
2. Ropes (or rope ladders) of sufficient length to reach ground level from site windows.
3. A standard first aid kit.

Wolfson further recommends that each employee have these items always at hand:

1. Flashlight (with extra batteries)
2. Bottled water (1 day supply)
3. Gas mask and charcoal canister

While many authorities concur with Wolfson, Inga Maund[2] stresses two further defenses against radiation:

1. Radiation-shield tables
2. Iosat pills (1 day supply per employee)

Regarding company-wide preparedness, several sources recommend the use of walkie-talkies, with a range of at least five miles, to maintain communication among divisions.

[1]Robert Wolfson, *Workplace Security in an Age of Bioterrorism* (New York: Alert Books, 2002), pp. 95–6.

[2]Inga Maund, "Dirty Bombs: Defending Our Own," *Managers Weekly* (April 6, 2003), p. 46.

Figure 12–8
Formal Report—Sample Body Page

25

CONCLUSION AND RECOMMENDATIONS

On the basis of information in this report it can be concluded that:

1. Pre-hire screening and background checks are currently being performed but are limited in scope to educational, employment, and criminal histories.
2. Post-hire security checks are not being conducted.
3. Security thoroughly screens personnel entering the facility. Packages and materials arriving by mail or courier are not screened.
4. Only Research and Development has a plan for responding to chemical and/or biological contamination. The only other existing response plans are based on fire evacuation procedures.
5. No plan exists for communicating with appropriate authorities or outside agencies or for continuing company operations after an "event."

From these conclusions, it is therefore recommended that:

1. Personnel immediately begin expanding applicant background checks as well as instituting regular follow-up security checks on current employees.
2. Shipping and Receiving immediately begin researching the necessary package-screening equipment to secure all mail and deliveries entering the facility. Required funding be made available immediately. The possibility of relocating the department off-site should be considered.
3. Each division develop a response plan, to be approved by management, including evacuation and/or containment procedures, "cleanup" requirements, and training in these procedures for all employees.
4. Management begin identifying and reserving an alternative site from which to continue operations. Management also should establish lines of communication with outside agencies to be notified in the case of an "event."

Figure 12–9
Formal Report—Conclusion and Recommendations

26

APPENDICES

APPENDIX 1

BUILDING PREPARATION:
WALK-THROUGH CHECKLIST

CONDITION OF EQUIPMENT

☐ Is all mechanical equipment in functioning order?
☐   appropriately connected?
☐   sufficiently controlled?

☐ Are all access doors and panels in place?
☐   sealed?

AIR SYSTEM

☐ How does air flow through the building?
☐ How is the building zoned?
☐ Are there handlers for each zone?
☐ What are the pressure relationships between zones?
☐ Is a filtration system in place?
☐ Is it operating efficiently?
☐ Are all dampers functioning?
☐ Are supply and return ducts completely connected?
☐   responsive to control?
☐ Are utility chases, elevator shafts, and stairwells significant air-flow paths?

OUTSIDE ACCESS

☐ Is the building connected to others by tunnel?
☐   by passageway?
☐ Do adjacent buildings allow roof access?
☐ Does landscaping allow undetected access?
☐ Are there outside louvers?
☐ Are they visible to the public?
☐   accessible to the public?

Figure 12–10
Formal Report—Appendix

28

BIBLIOGRAPHY

advisories.homelandsecurity.gov

Capoccia, Paula. "The Role of the Infectious Disease Team in the Post 9/11
World." *Journal of the International Medical Association*, vol. X,
issue 4, June 2003, pp. 62–78.

Kovacs, Thomas, M.D. *Bioterrorism: Fact from Fiction.* New York: Red
Guides, 2003.

Maund, Inga. "Dirty Bombs: Defending Our Own." *Managers Weekly*,
April 6, 2003, pp. 43–50.

Wolfson, Robert. *Workplace Security in an Age of Bioterrorism.* New York:
Alert Books, 2002.

Figure 12–11
Formal Report—Bibliography

3. *Illustration*—The body of your report can be substantiated by the use of charts, graphs, tables, diagrams, and photographs. These should be used to present data not easily expressed in prose; they should not be used to repeat data already presented in your text. Each illustration should be labeled and, if many are included, numbered as well.

Finally, you must be sure to cite your sources! When you quote another person's words and ideas, you must say so. Failure to do this constitutes **plagiarism**, which is essentially information theft. If you interview people, name them. If you refer to books, articles, or web sites, footnote them (see #6 in the list that begins below). You lose no credit when you acknowledge the source of your information, but you lose all credibility (and maybe even your job) if you are caught presenting another person's ideas as your own.

When your report is complete and ready to be printed, keep in mind these guidelines for preparing the manuscript:

1. Use *standard manuscript form*—double space on one side of 8½ × 11″ paper.
2. *Number every page*—except the title page—in the upper right-hand corner.
3. Leave lots of *white space*—allow ample margins as well as space between subtopics.
4. Use lots of *headings and subheadings*—make your report logical by giving headings of equal weight parallel wording; surround headings with white space.
5. Pay attention to *paragraphing*—try to keep your paragraphs more or less equal in length. (A paragraph of 15 lines should not be followed by one of 6 lines; on the other hand, paragraphs of 15 and

11 lines, although unequal, would not be too unbalanced.) Also, give each paragraph, like the report as a whole, a logical structure; start with a topic sentence and follow with supporting details.

6. Be sure to *footnote* information that you take from other sources— quotations should be followed by a raised number[1] and at the bottom of the page a notation should be made:

   [1]Helen J. McLane, *Selecting, Developing and Retaining Women Executives* (New York: Van Nostrand Reinhold, 2002), pp. 71–73.

7. *Proofread* your report for errors in grammar, spelling, capitalization, and punctuation.
8. Bind the finished manuscript securely.

Proposals

A proposal (Figures 12–12 and 12–13) is a sales pitch for an idea. Its purpose is to persuade someone to go along with your idea and put it into action.

Proposals are required in a variety of situations. For example, you may want to

- suggest an idea to your employer to change a company procedure, hire an additional employee, purchase new equipment, and so on;
- recommend an idea or project to a committee or board;
- apply for a grant to fund a project;
- solicit financial backing from investors for a new business or project;
- solicit a contract from a potential customer or client.

The information you include and the format you choose for your proposal will vary with the situation. Some proposals, particularly grant applications, require the completion of extensive application forms and must follow a format prescribed by the organization offering the grant. In any case, all proposals must meet certain criteria:

1. *Define your idea.* Early in the proposal you must state **clearly** your actual idea. You must define its purpose, as well as its scope and limitations. If you are presenting the idea to people unfamiliar with the background for the idea, you must fill them in, creating a context in which the idea fits logically.
2. *Be persuasive.* Offer specific reasons for your idea, including the benefits or advantages to be gained from it. Present these reasons logically, not just as a list but as an organized progression that gradually builds an irrefutable case for your idea.
3. *Anticipate objections.* Provide answers to questions or doubts before they are raised. This may include credentials of people involved, justification of costs or expenditures, or refutation of alternative ideas.
4. *Explain how to proceed.* What must be done to implement your idea? What would you like your reader to do? Is there a deadline by which a decision must be made?

PARMA REFRIGERATOR & STOVE CO., INC.   Sales & Service

1500 Wellman Square   PHONE   800-555-1234
Bronx, New York 10481   FAX   718-555-4567

PROPOSAL
Bid to Provide Appliances Under HUD Guidelines

TO: Federation of Latino Communities, Inc.
          Bedford Paraiso SRO Program
          5000 Bedford Park Row
          Bronx, New York 10492

ATT: Fernando Lebron

FROM: Angela Parma Stern
          Vice President

DATE: April 18, 20—

   Based on a bulk order, single delivery and all installations
being completed in one day, we can provide the appliances you
specified at the following discount:

- 22 Federal Electric all-electric stoves, Mod. No. ES02V
  delivered and installed @ $420 each $9,240.00
- 48 Federal Electric 30" ductless range hoods, Mod. No. RH32
  delivered and installed @ $66 each $3,168.00
- Parts for Federal Electric cooktop, Mod. No. CT201B
  44 6" burners @ $20 each, delivered only ....$ 880.00
  44 8" burners @ $25 each, delivered only $1,100.00
  22 burner receptacles @ $9.50 each, delivered only $ 209.00

TOTAL: $14,597.00

TERMS: • 20% ($2,919.40) retainer due upon signing of contract
         (certified check)
       • Balance ($11,677.60) due upon delivery (certified check)

ADDITIONAL CRITERIA: (1) All merchandise is covered by a
                          manufacturer's 1-full-year warranty.
                     (2) We carry $2 million liability insurance.
                     (3) All members of our crew are union members
                          with prior experience on HUD projects.
                     (4) We conform to all regulations of the
                          Davis-Bacon Act regarding hiring practices.

All items are available for immediate shipment. We can process
your order as soon as we hear from you.

Figure 12–12
Proposal I

A PROPOSAL TO HOLD AN IN-HOUSE CONFERENCE ON DIGITAL MEDIA AND SOCIAL NETWORKING

WHAT WE WOULD LIKE TO SOLVE

Over the last three to five years, social media have gone beyond their original purpose as communication links among personal acquaintances and friends. They have now become places of business. We have fallen behind our competitors in using social media as a tool, not just for marketing but for networking with our customers and business partners. Our problem is two-edged: our younger, digital media-savvy employees do not think of social networks as a business environment; many of our more experienced senior employees are unfamiliar with social networking and are in effect digitally illiterate.

WHAT WE PROPOSE TO DO

We would hold, on a Saturday, a one-day in-house conference on digital media and social networking. Three local colleges offer continuing education courses in digital media, and several faculty members at each school are available for outside speaking engagements. During the morning, we will schedule three lectures: "The Language of Social Media," "The Future of Social Networking in the Business World," and "Integrating Social Media at Our Company." In the afternoon, we will run several workshops in such areas as setting up a Twitter account, using Facebook for content creation and sharing, and creating photo profiles. Employees will be encouraged to attend those workshops that most suit their own needs and job description.

WHAT BENEFITS WE WILL ACHIEVE

The benefits will occur in most departments.

1. Marketing will benefit by learning to promote our company by establishing its online corporate identity via accounts with various social networks. By developing tools such as blogging and podcasting, they will expand the reach of our marketing efforts.
2. Sales will benefit from Marketing's enhanced work and will also learn to establish online relationships with our customers. Each sales representative will learn to "live" in an online community, keeping our clients informed and up-to-date on our products and services, as well as encouraging feedback.
3. Employees throughout the company will benefit by becoming part of the company's online identity. They will learn that social networking is not just a personal activity; they will discover the business consequences of their online profiles, for both their own careers as well as the company's image. Additionally, increased job skills will increase job satisfaction, which in turn increases productivity.
4. The company as a whole will benefit when we create an online corporate identity on a par with our competitors. By raising the digital media skills of our entire staff and engaging everyone in the maintenance of our corporate image, we will then surpass our competitors.

WHAT THIS WILL COST
The main cost will be the speakers' fees for the visiting lecturers. We anticipate that they will cost between $5,000 and $7,500 each. By using graduate students as workshop leaders, we will be able to keep those costs down to $500 each; we expect to run six to ten workshops.

Facility costs will only be for Saturday staffing since we will hold the conference in-house (the conference room for the morning lectures, six to ten offices for the afternoon workshops). We expect to require two security guards (one in the lobby, one on our floor) and two custodial workers (for setup and cleanup), all at time and a half. Building management advises us that this will cost $800–$1,000.

Therefore, total costs will be $8,800–$13,500.

WHAT HAPPENS NEXT
With the approval of the proposal we will
1. Contact the deans of continuing education at each local college for the names of faculty members available for speaking engagements. We will contact those instructors with the lecture topics we are planning and the speaker's fee we are offering. From the instructors who respond, we will select three.
2. Solicit, from the selected lecturers, names of graduate students to run the afternoon workshops. From the responses, we will select six to ten whose proposed topics suit our needs.
3. Coordinate with our office building's management to schedule the custodial and security staff required to keep the building open on the designated Saturday.
4. Notify our own employees of the event, providing a month's notice for them to make themselves available on a Saturday.

We are ready to institute the proposal as soon as we receive an executive decision.

Figure 12–13 (Continued)
Proposal II

The size of your idea will determine the length of your proposal. If you are proposing the purchase of new furniture for your reception area, you will need a briefer rationale than you would for a proposal for a bank loan to start up a new business. Still, all proposals must have the following:

- TITLE: This should be terse but clearly identify your idea.
- HEADINGS: Divide your persuasive argument into subtitled sections. You will make your proposal easier to read and your rationale easier to follow.

A long proposal may also include:

- SUMMARY: At the beginning, you will provide the busy executive with a synopsis of your idea and main supporting points.

- APPENDICES: Substantiating data can be attached at the end. Appendices may include résumés of the people involved in the project, tables and charts of financial figures or other relevant statistics, and any other information that would interrupt the flow of your persuasive argument but is nevertheless essential to the proposal.
- COVER: A long proposal should be bound in a plastic or cardboard cover.

Finally, you must consider the tone of your proposal. You want the *logic* of your idea to predominate, supported by specific facts and information, but you must also convey your own enthusiasm for the idea. You must communicate a sense of urgency if you want your reader to act. We began by saying a proposal is a sales pitch, and you will not successfully pitch an idea you don't believe in.

PRACTICE CORRESPONDENCE

The following activities require that you prepare either a formal or an informal report. Be sure to employ an appropriate format.

A. Your employer has requested the latest closing prices on the following stocks (both preferred and common):

AT&T	General Motors
Microsoft	IBM
Exxon	Facebook

Consult a newspaper or the Internet for the necessary information and present the data in an informal report.

B. A strike of the local transit workers union is anticipated in your community. In order to be prepared, your employer has asked you to investigate the cost of renting hotel rooms for the chief executives of the company. Contact a number of local hotels to find out their daily and weekly rates. Then present this information in an informal report. Include your recommendation for the most economical and convenient place to stay.

C. The budget for your department in the coming fiscal quarter includes funds for the purchase of two-way radios for the outside technical staff. Your supervisor wants to purchase equipment that is both state-of-the-art and appropriate for department needs. Prepare a report comparing at least four different brands of two-way radios currently on the market. Compare the brands by price and service histories. Consider differences in such features as channels and subcodes, talk button location and button lock, transmitter cut-off and auto squelch, vibrate alert, and low-battery indicator.

D. The Counseling Department of the Fort Worth Business Institute has been establishing transfer-of-credit agreements with other educational institutions in the region. As the school's assistant director of counseling, prepare a formal report detailing the course requirements for the major programs of study in your school. Include a brief description of the course content and the number of credits awarded for each course.

E. Your local school board is seeking to raise funds to expand the high school library. It has turned to the business community for fund-raising ideas. As a local business owner, you would like to suggest a town fair to be held in the school yard on a Saturday. Because local businesses as well as private citizens could rent space from the school board to run booths or games, the entire community could be involved in such a fund-raising activity. Write a proposal to the school board suggesting your idea for a town fair. When you present your plan of action, be sure to include persuasive reasons for your idea. Also be sure to anticipate possible objections.

Last Details

The final section of this book is intended to help you put some of the finishing touches on your correspondence. "A Glossary of Business Terms," though by no means exhaustive, will help you make certain that you are using specialized words in their proper business sense. "Addressing Dignitaries" will provide you with acceptable terms of address for individuals of rank. (The reader is advised, however, that such terms are a matter of custom and vary widely with locale.) "Some Grammar Basics," "Punctuation," "Capitalizaiton," "Abbreviations," and "Numbers" provide, in outline form, an overview of the basic rules of English mechanics.

A Glossary of Business Terms

account *n.* (1) a bookkeeping record of business transactions; (2) a customer or client.

accrue *v.* to accumulate, as interest.

affidavit *n.* a written oath.

amortization *n.* the gradual paying off of a debt at regular intervals.

annuity *n.* an investment that provides fixed yearly payments.

appraise *v.* to evaluate.

appreciate *v.* to increase in value.

arbitration *n.* settlement of a dispute through a third party.

arrears *n.* overdue debts.

assessment *n.* evaluation for the purpose of taxation.

asset *n.* something that is owned and has value.

audit (1) *n.* the checking of a business's financial records. (2) *v.* to check a business's financial records.

backup (1) *v.* to copy a file from a computer hard drive to floppy disks or tapes. (2) *n.* a duplicate copy of a computer file.

balance (1) *n.* the difference between debits and credits. (2) *v.* to reconcile the difference between debits and credits.

bankruptcy *n.* the legally declared state of being unable to pay debts.

beneficiary *n.* a person stipulated to receive benefits from a will, insurance policy, etc.

bond *n.* a long-term debt security issued by a public or private borrower.

boot *v.* to turn on a computer.

brokerage *n.* a business licensed to sell stocks and securities.

byte *n.* a measure of computer capacity to store information, one byte being equivalent to one character.

capacity *n.* the total number of bytes that can be stored in a computer's memory.

capital *n.* money or property owned or used by a business.

cash flow *n.* a measure of a company's liquidity.

CD-ROM *n.* acronym for Compact Disk Read-Only Memory, an optical computer storage device containing millions of bytes of information.

collateral *n.* property used as security for a loan.

compensation *n.* payment, reimbursement.

consignment *n.* shipment of goods to be paid for after they are sold.

corporation *n.* a business operating under a charter.

credit (1) *n.* the entry of a payment in an account. (2) *v.* to enter a payment in an account.

data processing *n.* the handling of information, especially statistical information, by computer.

debit (1) *n.* the entry of money owed in an account. (2) *v.* to enter money owed in an account.

debt *n.* money owed.

debug *v.* to remove errors from a computer program.

deficit *n.* a money shortage.

depreciate *v.* to decrease in value.

direct mail *n.* the sale of goods and services through the mail.

dividend *n.* a share of profits divided among the stockholders of a corporation.

download *v.* to move information from the memory of one computer to that of another or to a tape, disk, or printer.

endorse *v.* to sign the back of a check.

endowment *n.* money given, as a bequest.

equity *n.* the amount of money no longer owed on a purchase.

escrow *n.* written evidence of ownership held by a third party until specified conditions are met.

executor *n.* a person named to carry out someone else's will.

exemption *n.* money not subject to taxation.

expenditure *n.* an amount of money spent.

fiscal *adj.* financial.

flextime *n.* a system of flexible work hours.

forfeiture *n.* loss of property as a penalty for default or neglect.

franchise *n.* a special right to operate a business granted by the government or a corporation.

goodwill *n.* the value of a business's public image and reputation.

gross (1) *adj.* total, before deductions. (2) *v.* to earn a certain amount before deductions. (3) *n.* the total before deductions. (4) *n.* twelve dozen.

hardware *n.* the physical machinery of a computer.

information processing *n.* the "marriage" of data processing and word processing.

input *n.* data fed into a computer.

insurance *n.* the guarantee of compensation for a specified loss.

interest *n.* (1) the fee charged for borrowing money; (2) money earned on an investment.

inventory *n.* an itemized list of property or merchandise.

investment *n.* money put into a business or transaction to reap a profit.

invoice *n.* a list of goods shipped.

journal *n.* a written record of financial transactions.

kilobyte *n.* approximately 1000 bytes.

laptop *n.* a compact, portable computer.

lease (1) *n.* a contract for renting property. (2) *v.* to rent or let.

ledger *n.* a record book of debits and credits.

legacy *n.* money or property left in a will.

liability *n.* a debt or obligation.

lien *n.* a claim on property as security against a debt.

liquidity *n.* ability to turn assets into cash.

list price *n.* retail price as listed in a catalog.

load *v.* to move information into a computer's memory.

margin *n.* difference between cost and selling price.

markup *n.* the percentage by which selling price is more than the cost.

megabyte *n.* approximately 1 million bytes.

memory *n.* information stored in a computer.

merger *n.* the combining of two or more companies into one.

middleman *n.* a businessperson who buys from a producer and resells at wholesale or retail in smaller quantities.

modem *n.* a device for linking computers by telephone line or cable.

monetary *adj.* relating to money.

monopoly *n.* exclusive control of a commodity or service.

mortgage (1) *n.* the pledging of property as security for a loan. (2) *v.* to pledge property as security for a loan.

negotiable *adj.* transferable.

net (1) *n.* an amount left after deductions. (2) *v.* to clear as profit.

networking *n.* the establishing of business and professional contacts.

option *n.* the right to act on an offer at an established price within a limited time.

output *n.* data provided by a computer.

overhead *n.* the costs of running a business.

par value *n.* the face value of a share of stock or a bond.

payable *adj.* owed.

personnel *n.* employees, staff.

petty cash *n.* money kept on hand for incidental purchases.

portfolio *n.* the various securities held by an investor.

power of attorney *n.* the written right to legally represent another person.

premium *n.* a payment, usually for an insurance policy.

productivity *n.* rate of yield or output.

proprietor *n.* owner.

prospectus *n.* a statement describing a business.

proxy *n.* authorization to vote for a stockholder at a meeting.

quorum *n.* the minimum number of persons required to be present for the transaction of business at a meeting.

receivable *adj.* due.

remittance *n.* the sending of money in payment.

requisition *n.* a written request for supplies.

résumé *n.* an outline of a job applicant's qualifications and experience.

rider *n.* an amendment to a document.

royalty *n.* a share of the profits from a book or invention paid to the author or patent holder.

security *n.* (1) funds or property held as a pledge of repayment; (2) a stock or bond.

shareholder *n.* one who owns shares of a corporation's stock.

software *n.* set of programs for a computer.

solvent *adj.* able to pay debts.

spreadsheet *n.* a table of numbers arranged in rows and columns for computer calculations.

stockholder *n.* one who owns stock in a company.

subsidy *n.* a monetary grant.

tariff *n.* a tax on imports or exports.

telecommunications *n.* high-speed communications via wire or microwave.

trust *n.* a monopoly formed by a combination of corporations.

turnaround time *n.* time taken to complete a task.

word processing *n.* the handling of narrative information by computer.

Addressing Dignitaries

CLERGY	
Term of Address	**Mode of Salutation**

(Alternatives are listed in order of decreasing formality.)

Abbot
The Right Reverend Abbot Scott
  (*plus the initials of his order*)

Right Reverend and Dear Father:
Dear Father Abbott:

Archbishop
The Most Reverend John P. Doohan
Archibishop of (*place name*)

Your Excellency:
Your Grace:

Archdeacon
The Venerable the Archdeacon of
  (*place name*)

Venerable Sir:

The Venerable Walter Frank
Archdeacon of (*place name*)

Bishop (Anglican)
The Right Reverend the Lord
Bishop of (*place name*)

My Lord Bishop:
My Lord:

The Lord Bishop of (*place name*)

Bishop (Methodist)
The Reverend Aaron Jones
Bishop of (*place name*)

Reverend Sir:
Dear Sir:
Dear Bishop Jones:

Bishop (Protestant Episcopal)
The Right Reverend Thomas Watt
Bishop of (*place name*)

Right Reverend Sir:
Dear Bishop Watt:

Bishop (Roman Catholic)
The Most Reverend Samuel Keen
Bishop of (*place name*)

Your Excellency:

Bishop (Scottish)
The Right Reverend Bishop Alan Crane

Right Reverend Sir:

Canon
The Very Reverend Canon John Steed

Very Reverend Canon:
Dear Canon Steed:

The Very Reverend John Steed
Canon of (*place name*)

Cardinal

His Eminence Ralph Cardinal Peel

His Eminence Cardinal Peel

Your Eminence:

Cardinal/Archbishop

His Eminence the Cardinal,
  Archibishop of (*place name*)

His Eminence Cardinal Pierce,
  Archibishop of (*place name*)

Your Eminence:

Clergyman or Clergywoman

The Reverend Richard North

Dear Sir:

The Reverend Dr. Priscilla North
  (*if Doctor of Divinity*)

Dear Dr. North:

Dean (Ecclesiastical)

The Very Reverend the Dean of
  St. John's

The Very Reverend William Hart

Sir:
Very Reverend Sir:
Very Reverend Father:
  (*Roman Catholic*)

Monsignor

The Right Reverend Monsignor
  Horace Wall

The Right Reverend and
  Dear Monsignor:
The Right Reverend Monsignor
  Horace Wall:
Dear Monsignor Wall:

Mother Superior

The Reverend Mother, Superior
Convent of (*name*)

Mother Mary Frances, Superior
Convent of (*name*)

The Reverend Mother Mary Frances
  (*plus initials of her order*)

Reverend Mother:
Dear Madam:
Dear Reverend Mother:
Dear Reverend Mother Mary
  Frances:

Nun

Sister Mary Theresa (*plus initials of
  her order*)

Dear Sister:
Dear Sister Mary Theresa:

Pope

His Holiness Pope Benedict XVI

His Holiness the Pope

Most Holy Father:
Your Holiness:

Priest (Episcopal)
The Reverend William Long   Dear Father Long:

Priest (Roman Catholic)
The Reverend Father Anthony Roma   Reverend Father:
  (plus initials of his order)   Dear Father Roma:

1) Benedictine, Cisterican, or Canon Regular   Reverend Father:
   The Very Reverend Dom Anthony Roma   Dear Father Roma:
     (plus initials of his order)

2) Carthusian   Venerable Father:
   The Venerable Father Anthony Roma,   Dear Father Roma:
   O. Cart.

3) Secular   Reverend Sir:
   The Reverend Anthony Roma   Dear Sir:
     (plus initials of his order)   Dear Father Roma:

Rabbi
Rabbi Hyman Marcus   Reverend Sir:
                                                         Dear Sir:
The Reverend Hyman Marcus   Dear Rabbi Marcus:
                                                         Dear Dr. Marcus:
Dr. Hyman Marcus

MILITARY	
Term of Address	**Mode of Salutation**
Admiral	
The Admiral of the Navy of the United States	Dear Sir:
Admiral Frank Scrod Chief of Naval Operations	Dear Admiral Scrod:
Brigadier General	
Brigadier General David P. Small	Dear Sir: Dear General Small:
Captain	
Captain Jesse Jones (*plus branch of military*)	Dear Sir: Dear Captain Jones:
Colonel	
Colonel Nathan Borman (*plus branch of military*)	Dear Sir: Dear Colonel Borman:
Commander	
Commander Morris Rosen United States Navy	Dear Sir: Dear Commander Rosen:
General	
General Jose Jerez United States Army	Sir: Dear Sir: Dear General Jerez:
Lieutenant Colonel	
Lieutenant Colonel Albert Robb United States Army	Dear Sir: Dear Colonel Robb:
Lieutenant General	
Lieutenant General Robert Howe	Dear Sir: Dear General Howe:
Major	
Major Susan Savan United States Army	Dear Madam: Dear Major Savan:
Major General	
Major General Clarence King United States Army	Dear Sir: Dear General King:
Rear Admiral	
Rear Admiral Evan Wyeth United States Navy	Dear Sir: Dear Admiral Wyeth:

GOVERNMENT/POLITICS

Term of Address	**Mode of Salutation**
Alderman or Alderwoman Alderman Clark Cook	Dear Sir or Madam: Dear Alderman Cook:
The Honorable Clark Cook Alderman	
Ambassador (American) The American Ambassador to 　(*place name*)	Sir: Your Excellency: Dear Madam Ambassador:
The American Embassy (*place name*)	
The Honorable Carol Eames The American Ambassador to (*place name*)	
Ambassador (Foreign) His Excellency The Ambassador of (*place name*)	Sir: Excellency: Your Excellency:
(*Place name*) Embassy Washington, D.C.	
His Excellency Christopher Latour Ambassador of (*place name*)	
Assemblyman or Assemblywoman The Honorable Marianne Glace Member of Assembly	Dear Madam: Dear Ms. Glace:
Assemblywoman Marianne Glace	
Associate Justice of the Supreme Court The Honorable Ruth Bader Ginsberg Associate Justice of the Supreme Court	Madam: Madam Justice: Your Honor:
The Honorable Ruth Bader Ginsberg Justice, Supreme Court of the United States	Dear Justice Ginsberg:
Cabinet Officer The Honorable Kevin Black Secretary of (*department name*)	Sir: Dear Sir: Dear Mr. Secretary:
The Secretary of (*title*)	

Chief Justice of the United States

The Honorable John Roberts
Chief Justice of the Supreme Court
  of the United States

Chief Justice Roberts
United States Supreme Court

The Chief Justice of the United States

Sir:
Mr. Chief Justice:
Dear Justice Roberts:

Commissioner

The Honorable Thelma Dole
Commissioner of (*bureau name*)

Madam:
Dear Madam:
Dear Ms. Dole:

Congressman or Congresswoman

The Honorable Stuart Larson
House of Representatives

The Honorable Stuart Larson
Representative in Congress
  (*when out of Washington*)

Representative Stuart Larson
House of Representatives

Sir:
Dear Sir:
Dear Congressman Larson:
Dear Representative Larson:
Dear Mr. Larson:

Consul

Miss Rhonda Marley
United States Consul at (*place name*)

Dear Madam:

Governor

His Excellency
The Governor of (*state name*)

The Honorable the Governor of
  (*state name*)

The Honorable Howard Brown
Governor of (*state name*)

Sir:
Dear Sir:
Dear Governor Brown:

Judge

The Honorable Laura Gordon
Judge of the Circuit Court
  (*or other title*)

Dear Madam:
Dear Judge Gordon:

Lieutenant Governor

The Honorable Sydney Blunt
Lieutenant Governor of (*state name*)

Sir:
Dear Sir:
Dear Mr. Blunt:

Mayor
The Mayor of (*place name*)   Sir:
Dear Sir:

The Honorable Lawrence O'Rourke   Dear Mr. Mayor:
Mayor of (*place name*)   Dear Mayor O'Rourke:

Minister (Diplomatic)
The Honorable Bertram Blyth   Sir:
Minister of (*place name*)   Dear Mr. Minister:

President of the United States
The President   Mr. President:
The White House   Dear Mr. President:

Senator
The Honorable Chester L. Fried   Dear Sir:
United States Senator   Dear Senator Fried:

The Honorable Regina Lukas   Dear Senator Lukas:
The Senate of (*state name*)

Speaker of the House
The Honorable Thomas Southey   Mr. Speaker:
Speaker of the House of Representatives   Dear Mr. Southey:

Vice-President of the United States
The Vice-President of the United States   Mr. Vice-President:
United States Senate   Sir:

The Honorable Gary Cross
Vice-President of the United States

NOBILITY

Term of Address	Mode of Salutation
Baron	
The Right Honorable Lord Chichester	My Lord:
	Dear Lord Chichester:
The Lord Chichester	
Baroness	
The Right Honorable Lady Chichester	Madam:
	Dear Lady Chichester:
The Lady Chichester	
Baronet	
Sir Richard Bartlett, Bart.	Sir:
Countess	
The Right Honorable the Countess of (*place name*)	Madam:
	Dear Lady (*place name*):
Duchess	
Her Grace the Duchess of (*place name*)	Madam:
	Your Grace:
Duke	
His Grace the Duke of (*place name*)	My Lord Duke:
	Your Grace:
Earl	
The Right Honorable the Earl of (*place name*)	My Lord:
King	
The King's Most Excellent Majesty	Sir:
	May it please your Majesty:
His Most Gracious Majesty King John	
Knight	
Sir Edward Leigh (*plus initials of his order*)	Sir:
	Dear Sir Edward:
Queen	
The Queen's Most Excellent Majesty	Madam:
	May it please your Majesty:
Her Gracious Majesty, The Queen	

Some Grammar Basics

THE SENTENCE

A Sentence is a group of words containing at least one verb and its subject.

> Jake <u>prepared</u> the report
> Subject   verb

A. The *verb* is the part of the sentence that indicates what someone or something DOES or IS or HAS.

> My accountant <u>filled</u> out my income tax return.
> Her method <u>is</u> more efficient than mine.
> She <u>has</u> a lot of information to save me money.

B. The *subject* is the part of the sentence that indicates who or what is "doing" the verb.

1) The subject can be a NOUN (a person, place, thing, or idea).

> <u>Carmen</u> is a hedge fund manager.

2) Or the subject can be a PRONOUN (a substitute for a noun to avoid repetition).

> <u>She</u> likes her job.

C. There are four basic sentence patterns.

1) <u>Subject</u> <u>verb</u>.

> <u>Chipper</u> <u>invested</u> in real estate.

2) <u>Subject</u> <u>verb</u> and <u>verb</u>.

> <u>Chipper</u> <u>saved</u> money and <u>invested</u> in real estate.

3) <u>Subject</u> and <u>subject</u> <u>verb</u>.

> <u>Chipper</u> and <u>Carole</u> <u>saved</u> money.

4) <u>Subject</u> and <u>subject</u> <u>verb</u> and <u>verb</u>.

> <u>Chipper</u> and <u>Carole</u> <u>saved</u> money and <u>invested</u> in real estate.

D. There are three more complicated sentence patterns.

1) Combine two basic sentences with a semicolon.

> Chipper invested in real estate; Carole bought a bar.

2) Combine two basic sentences with a comma followed by a coordinating conjunction (*and, but, or, nor, for, so, yet*).

> Chipper invested in real estate, but Carole bought a bar.

3) Combine two basic sentences by using a subordinating conjunction:

W   who, what, where, when, why, which, whether, while
I   if
S   since, so that
H   how

A   as, as if, after, although
B   before, because
O   once
U   unless, until
T   than, that, till, though

a)   Combine two basic sentences by inserting a subordinating conjunction between them.

> Chipper invested in real estate whole Carole bought a bar.

b)   Combine two basic sentences by inserting a comma between them and using a subordinating conjunction as the first word of the new sentence.

> Although Chipper invested in real estate, Carole bought a bar.

E.   There are two basic sentence errors.

1)   Fragment (an incomplete sentence)

a)   A subject but no verb

> Carole, an experienced personnel manager.

b)   A verb but no subject

> Handled her staff adeptly.

c)   A subordinating conjunction attached to the only subject and verb

> Because Carole, an experienced personnel manager, handled her staff adeptly.

d)   *Correction:* Attach the fragment to a good sentence placed either before or after it.

> The bar was an immediate success because Carole, and experienced personnel manager, handled her staff adeptly.

(*or*)

> Because Carole, an experienced personnel manager, handled her staff adeptly, the bar was an immediate success.

e)   *Caution:* Present participles (*ing* words) look like verbs but aren't.

> Fragment: Carole, planning to expand the operation soon.

> Correction: Carole is planning to expand the operation soon.

2)   Run-on (two or more sentences incorrectly joined as one)

a)   Nothing used as a connection

> The real estate market slowed Chipper diversified into fine wines.

    b) Only a comma used as a conjunction

> The real estate market slowed, Chipper diversified into fine wines.

    c) *Correction:* Use a proper connection between the two sentences (see Section D).

- A semicolon

> The real estate market slowed; Chipper diversified into fine wines.

- A comma plus a coordinating conjunction

> The real estate market slowed, so Chipper diversified into fine wines.

- A subordinating conjunction

> The real estate marked slowed before Chipper diversified into fine wines.

- A comma between the parts and a subordinating conjunction as the first word of the new sentence

> After the real estate market slowed, Chipper diversified into fine wines.

    d) *Caution:* WORDS OF TRANSITION (such as *however* and *therefore*) are not subordinating conjunctions.

> Run-on: Investment wines are highly perishable, however Chipper stores them properly.
>
> Correction: Investment wines are highly perishable. However, Chipper stores them properly.

SUBJECT-VERB AGREEMENT

In the present tense, the verb and its subject in a sentence must "agree."

A. The basic rule of agreement: Only the verb *or* its subject (not both) may end in *s*.

> The receptionist answers the telephone.
> The receptionists answer the telephone.

B. Special cases

    1) Pronouns as subjects

      a) *He*, *she*, *it*, or *this* takes a verb with an *s*.

> He answers the phone with enthusiasm.

      b) *I*, *you*, *we*, *they*, *these*, and *those* take verbs with no *s*.

> They answer the phone professionally.

    2) Compound subjects (two or more nouns or pronouns connected by and) take a verb with no *s*.

> The treasurer works hard.
> Her assistant works hard.
>
> (*but*)
>
> The treasurer and her assistant work hard.

Note: In each of the following sentences the subject is singular, not plural or compound, and takes a singular verb.

Miss Burke, as well as her three assistants, <u>has</u> major responsibilities.
Miss Burke, along with her three assistants, <u>has</u> major responsibilities.
Miss Burke, aided by her three assistants, <u>has</u> major responsibilities.
Miss Burke, not her three assistants, <u>has</u> major responsibilities.

3) OR and NOR: When the nouns or pronouns in the subject are connected by *or* or *nor*, the verb must agree with the noun or pronoun closest to it.

My secretary or my assistant screen<u>s</u> my calls.
My secretary or my assistant<u>s</u> screen my calls.
Neither they nor he is coming.

4) TO BE: The present tense *and* the past tense have *s* forms.

Present: One broker <u>is</u> against the deal.
Three brokers <u>are</u> against the deal.

Past: One investor <u>was</u> convinced to buy.
Four investors <u>were</u> dissuaded from buying.

5) Well-described subjects: A group of words attached to the subject does not affect the verb.

The man <u>is</u> working hard.
The man at the controls <u>is</u> working hard.

The personal computer and a monitor cost $1200.

(*but*)

The personal computer with a monitor cost<u>s</u> $1200.

6) Irregular nouns as subjects: Some nouns in English are plural even though they don't end in *s*. As subjects, these plural nouns take a verb with no *s*.

The man seem<u>s</u> tired.
The men seem tired.

The woman <u>is</u> concerned.
The women are concerned.

The child look<u>s</u> frightened.
The children look frightened.

My foot hurt<u>s</u>.
My feet hurt.

7) Singular indefinite pronouns (*another, little, much, each, every*) take verbs with an *s*.

Little work remain<u>s</u> to be done.
Little remain<u>s</u> to be done.

Each person on the team <u>has</u> an assigned task.
Each <u>has</u> a strong sense of responsibility.

8) Collective nouns refer to a group of things or people as a single unit and so take verbs with an *s*.

> The class listen<u>s</u> attentively to the teacher.
> The army provide<u>s</u> extensive training to new recruits.

VERB TENSES

Verbs change form to indicate information about time.

A. Principal parts of the verb: Every verb has five principal parts:

	Example 1	*Example 2*
INFINITIVE	to walk	to go
PRESENT TENSE	walk, walks	go, goes
PAST TENSE	walked	went
PRESENT PARTICIPLE	walking	going
PAST PARTICIPLE	walked	gone

> **Note:** Of the five principal parts, only the *present tense* or the *past tense* can be the verb in a sentence. Each of the other parts needs a helping verb before it can be used as a verb in a sentence.

B. Tense formation: In addition to the present tense and the past tense, other tenses are formed by using one of the participles with a helping verb. The main helping verbs are TO BE and TO HAVE.

1)
Infinitive	to be	to have
Present Tense	is, are, am	has, have
Past Tense	was, were	had
Present Participle	being	having
Past Participle	been	had

2) *Perfect tenses* are formed by using the past participle with the present or past of *to have*.

- Angela <u>has worked</u> hard all her life.
- The guests <u>have arrived</u>.
- The project <u>had seemed</u> difficult before we started.

3) *Continuous tenses* are formed by using the present participle with the present or past of *to be*.

- The accountant <u>is trying</u> to concentrate.
- His clerks <u>are distracting</u> him.
- The journalists <u>were asking</u> questions.
- The politician <u>was avoiding</u> the answers.

4) *Perfect continuous tenses* require a present participle, the past participle of *to be* (*been*), and the present or past tense of *to have* as the helping verb.

- The actor <u>has been waiting</u>.
- The dancers <u>have been warming</u> up.
- The audience <u>had been expecting</u> a better performance.

5) *Future tenses* are formed by using *will* with an infinitive (without *to*).

will (to sing)	will sing
will (to be) singing	will be singing
will (to have) sung	will have sung
will (to have) been singing	will have been singing

- By the time the curtain falls, the soprano <u>will have been singing</u> for three hours.

C. Tense use: Tenses are used to express information about time. In addition to telling whether an event occurred in the past, present, or future, they show the time *relationship* between events, that is, whether one event happened before another or at the same time or even continuously over a period of time.

1) The simple tenses tell us the time frame of the main action.

- Today, Mr. Carrier <u>talks</u> to the Rotary Club.
- Last week, he <u>talked</u> to the Town Council.
- Next week, he <u>will talk</u> to the JayCees.

2) The continuous tenses refer to the same time as the simple tenses but tell that the action continued for a period of time.

- Today, Mr. Carrier <u>talks</u> to the Rotary Club.
- He <u>is talking</u> about the problem of local pollution.
- Last week, he <u>talked</u> to the Town Council.
- He <u>was talking</u> about the need for road repairs.
- Next week, he <u>will talk</u> to the JayCees.
- He <u>will be talking</u> about another public issue.

3) The perfect tenses are used for actions that don't coincide in time with the main action in the simple or continuous tense.

- Last week, Mr. Carrier <u>talked</u> to the Town Council.
- The week before, he <u>had talked</u> to the mayor about his speech. (FURTHER IN THE PAST)

- Last week, Mr. Carrier <u>talked</u> to the Town Council.
- Since then, he <u>has talked</u> privately to several council members. (BETWEEN THE PAST AND PRESENT)

- Mr. Carrier <u>will talk</u> to the JayCees next week.
- Before then, he <u>will have talked</u> to the mayor again. (BETWEEN THE PRESENT AND A LATER TIME IN THE FUTURE)

4) The perfect continuous tenses are used for actions that occur at approximately the same time as the perfect tense but continue over a period of time.

- Last week, Mr. Carrier <u>talked</u> to the Town Council.
- He <u>had been talking</u> to individual council members the week before.

- Today, he <u>talks</u> to the Rotary Club.
- He <u>has been talking</u> about his speech for days.

- He <u>will talk</u> to the JayCees next week.
- By then, he <u>will have been talking</u> to local groups for over a month.

D. Irregular verbs: Regular verbs form the past tense and past participle by adding an ED-ending to the infinitive without the *to*. Other verbs, however, are irregular and form the past tense and past participle by no consistent rule.

Some of the more commonly misused irregular verbs are:

Present Tense	Past Tense	Past Participle
arise	arose	arisen
bring	brought	brought
catch	caught	caught
choose	chose	chosen
do	did	done
drink	drank	drunk
eat	ate	eaten
lie	lied	lied
lie	lay	lain
lay	laid	laid
lose	lost	lost
pay	paid	paid
ring	rang	rung
see	saw	seen
set	set	set
sit	sat	sat
swim	swam	swum
take	took	taken
tear	tore	torn
write	wrote	written

PRONOUNS

Pronouns are substitutes for nouns, used to avoid purposeless repetition.

As soon as June arrived, <u>June</u> opened the store.
As soon as June arrived, <u>she</u> opened the store.

A. Case: Select your pronoun according to its function in the sentence.

1) NOMINATIVE CASE (if the pronoun is the subject of a verb)

a) Singular: *I, you, he, she, it, who*
b) Plural: *we, you, they, who*

- <u>Patricia</u> prepares all the paychecks.
- <u>She</u> prepares all the paychecks.

2) POSSESSIVE CASE (if the pronoun shows ownership. NOTE that none of these takes an apostrophe.)

a) Used with a following noun—singular: *my, your, his, her, its*
plural: *our, your, their*

     b) Used without a noun—singular: *mine, yours, his, hers, its*

                           plural: *ours, your, theirs*

- This book belongs to Ken and Joyce.
- It is <u>their</u> book.
- It is <u>theirs</u>.

3) OBJECTIVE CASE (if the pronoun is not a subject and does not show possession)

    a) Singular: *me, you, him, her, it*
    b) Plural: *us, you, them*

- I saw <u>Rosetta</u> at the meeting.
- I saw <u>her</u> at the meeting.

4) Difficult choices: Which case to use?

    a) In compound subjects or compound objects of verbs or prepositions

- Marc and (I, me) will plan the advertising.
- Marc and <u>I</u> <u>will plan</u> the advertising.

- The supervisor chose Marc and (I, me) to plan the advertising.
- The <u>supervisor</u> <u>chose</u> Marc and <u>me</u> to plan the advertising.

- The responsibility belongs to Marc and (I, me).
- The <u>responsibility</u> <u>belongs</u> to Marc and <u>me</u>.

    b) In subjects or objects linked by or

- Ms. Bayer or (I, me) will help you with your order.
- Ms. Bayer or <u>I</u> <u>will help</u> you with your order.

- At the meeting, Mr. Ames will name Jenny or (I, me).
- At the meeting, <u>Mr. Ames</u> <u>will name</u> Jenny or <u>me</u>.

- Joy prefers not to work with Nora or (he, him).
- <u>Joy</u> <u>prefers</u> not to work with Nora or <u>him</u>.

    c) Who, whom

- We hired the applicant (who, whom) was most qualified.
- We hired the applicant <u>who</u> <u>was</u> most qualified.

- The director did not care (who, whom) we hired.
- The director did not care <u>whom</u> <u>we</u> <u>hired</u>.

B. Agreement: A singular pronoun must be used to stand for a singular noun; a plural pronoun must be used to stand for a plural noun.

- The latest copy machine is very complex, and (they, it) is always breaking down.
- The latest copy <u>machine</u> is very complex, and <u>it</u> is always breaking down.

- Everyone has some job that (she, they) can do well.
- <u>Everyone</u> has some job that <u>she</u> can do well.

- Mrs. Leonard never made anyone feel that she was ordering (him, them) around.
- Mrs. Leonard never made <u>anyone</u> feel that she was ordering <u>him</u> around.

C. Reference

1) Do not use a pronoun unless the noun for which it stands has been mentioned previously.

- Since the legal profession is highly valued by the public, <u>they</u> are very well paid.

They?

- Since the legal profession is highly valued by the public, <u>lawyers</u> are very well paid.

(or)

- Since lawyers are highly valued by the public, <u>they</u> are very well paid.

2) Do not use a pronoun if it can be taken as a substitute for more than one noun.

- Annette met Lisa right after <u>she</u> left work.

She?

- Right after Annette left work, <u>she</u> met Lisa.

(or)

- Right after Lisa left work, Annette met <u>her</u>.

Punctuation

PERIOD

A. Use a period to mark the end of a sentence.

> Your inquiry has been received.

   1) Indirect questions are punctuated as sentences.

> You asked if we sell only to the trade.

   2) Commands are punctuated as sentences.

> Direct your questions to the manager of marketing.

   3) Requests are punctuated as sentences.

> Would you please let us know how we may be of further assistance.

B. Use a period to indicate an abbreviation.

> Mr.   Dr.   Inc.   Corp.
> Mrs.   Co.

Abbreviations of organizational names require *no* period.

> FBI   CIA   IBM   YMCA   NASA

C. DO NOT use a period

   1) after a heading or title

> Part Two: Know Your Customer

   2) after a sentence ending in a punctuated abbreviation

> I have spoken with the president of Remco, Inc.

   3) when the numbers or letters of a list have been enclosed in parentheses

> Please include the following:
>
> (1) Name
> (2) Address
> (3) Corporate affiliation

   4) after even amounts of dollars

> The price of $30 includes postage and handling.

   5) after a Roman numeral that is part of a name

> Ashley Hall III has sold her interest in our company.

EXCLAMATION POINT

A. Use an exclamation point, instead of a period, at the end of a sentence to indicate emphasis or strong emotion.

We will not be undersold!

B. Use an exclamation point after an interjection.

Wow! Did you see this month's sales figures?

QUESTION MARK

A. Use a question mark after a direct question.

Will the report be ready by the first of the month?

B. Use a question mark when directly quoting a question.

The accountant asked, "Did you incur any medical expenses this year?"

SEMICOLON

A. Use a semicolon to join two closely related sentences.

Our first task is to locate the error; the second is to correct it.

B. Use a semicolon to separate items in a series that are long or complex or have internal punctuation.

The firm received inquiries from some unfamiliar places: Engeli, Turkey; Erfurt, Germany; Kiruna, Switzerland; and Port Colborne, Canada.

COLON

A. Use a colon after a formal introductory statement or before such a statement as

1) a formal list

When evaluating a credit application, consider the following: credit history, employment history, and current assets.

2) an explanation

A letter refusing credit should be positive: you hope to continue business on a cash basis.

3) a quotation

A well-known financial consultant advises: "It is easier to establish credit before you need it."

B. Use a colon after the salutation in a business letter.

Dear Sirs:

C. Use a colon between a title and subtitle.

Online Sales: A Complete Guide for the Beginner

D. Use a colon between the hour and minutes of a time reference.

6:43 A.M.   9:40 P.M.

COMMA

A. Use a comma before a coordinating conjunction.

I will prepare the documents, and Mr. Russell will prepare the graphs.

B. Use a comma after an introductory subordinate clause.

Before we submit the project, we would like you to evaluate it.

C. Use a comma after an introductory element such as

1) a word of transition

Nevertheless, we are confident of our work.

2) an introductory phrase

After acceptance, the project will be put into effect promptly.

Having secured the account, Nancy celebrated with a fine dinner.

D. Use commas to separate items in a list.

It will require the cooperation of the sales representatives, secretarial staff, and department managers.

E. Use commas to set off interrupting expressions, including

1) contrasted elements

The president, not her assistant, will attend the meeting.

2) parenthetical expressions

This information, I am sure, will remain confidential.

3) appositives

My receptionist, Ms. Sanders, will give you an appointment.

4) explanatory expressions, such as

a) degrees and titles

Mario Piccolo, Ph.D., is author of the book under discussion.

    b) corporate abbreviations

        After leaving David Jonas, Ltd., he started his own company.

    c) state names

        Corporate headquarters has been moved from Indianapolis, Indiana, to Columbus, Ohio.

    d) years in date references

        The package was shipped on June 2, 2012, and arrived on June 5, 2012.

  5) nonrestrictive clauses

      My husband, who works faster than I, often helps me before a deadline.

F. Use a comma or commas to set off words in direct addresses.

    Dr. Long, I am here to introduce a new product.
    My feelings, dear friends, are too deep for words.

APOSTROPHE

A. Use an apostrophe to indicate possession.

    the profits of the company—the company's profits
    the investments of Rob—Rob's investment
    the obligation of everyone—everyone's obligation

    the role of the actress—the actress's role
    the work of Gus—Gus's work
    the benefits of the employees—the employees' benefits
    the meeting of the managers—the managers' meetings

B. Use the apostrophe in contractions.

    I had—I'd
    do not—don't
    we are—we're
    1968—'68

C. Use apostrophes to form special plurals.

  1) Lower case letters

      The *t*'s on the sign are all crooked.

  2) Abbreviations ending with periods.

      The G.I.'s were happy to be home.

QUOTATION MARKS

A. Use quotation marks to enclose direct quotations.

During her speech, Margaret Rome commented, "Real estate, while still a sound investment, will no longer reap the returns it has over the past decade."

B. Use quotation marks to enclose the titles of short works (stories, articles, essays, poems, and chapters). Underline the titles of full-length works (books, magazines, newspapers, plays, movies, and television shows).

Ms. Pierce's article, "Recognizing High-Growth Stocks," appeared in the January issue of *Making Money*.

C. Use quotation marks to enclose words used in a special sense.

"Interface," a word once familiar only to dressmakers and tailors, is now a cliché in corporate parlance.

HYPHEN

A. Use a hyphen to join two or more words in a compound.

Do-it-yourself books are often big sellers.

B. Use a hyphen with fractions and compound numbers from 21 to 99.

one-fifth   twenty-one
three-eighths   seventy-four

C. Use a hyphen with such prefixes as *ex-*, *all-*, *self-*, and *pro-*.

ex-wife   self-propelled
all-star   pro-tennis

D. Use a hyphen to divide a word, between syllables, at the end of a line.

Once a year, each employee's performance is methodi-
cally evaluated.

DASH

A. Use a dash to indicate an abrupt break in thought.

To get a new business off the ground takes hard work and determination—though a little luck helps.

B. Use a dash to break off an unfinished statement.

Mr. Morris muttered, "Where have I left my—"

C. Use a dash between an introductory list and the explanatory sentence that follows.

Calmness, confidence, and a copy of your resume—bring all of these with you to a job interview.

PARENTHESES

A. Use parentheses to enclose statements that are completely separate from the main thought of the sentence, such as

1) supplements

   In some professions (physical therapy, for example) a dress code may be strictly enforced.

2) references

   According to the union contract, all employees must have a high school diploma on file (see section 6, paragraph 1).

B. Use parentheses for enumeration within a sentence.

You will need the following: (1) your resume, (2) letters of reference, (3) a college transcript, and (4) a pad and pencil.

BRACKETS

A. Use brackets as parentheses within parentheses.

The role of business in American life has been the subject of our fiction (see, for example, the novels of William Dean Howells [1837–1920]).

B. Use brackets around interpolations within a quotation.

In *Death of a Salesman* by Arthur Miller, Charlie pays tribute to Willy Loman: "[A salesman's] a man way out there in the blue, riding on a smile and a shoe shine. . . . A salesman is got to dream, boy. It comes with the territory."

C. Use brackets around editorial comments and corrections.

The professor ended his lecture with this remark: "All of you will hopefully [*sic*] read at least some of these books." (Here *sic*, meaning literally "so" or "thus," signifies that the word *hopefully*, although used incorrectly, is being reproduced from the original quotation.)

Capitalization

A. Capitalize the first word of a sentence.

The man paid by check.

B. Capitalize the first word of a complete sentence within a sentence.

1) Quotations

   My advisor says, "It is never too early to plan your career."

2) Certain questions

   The real issue was, What were we to do about the problem?

3) Statements after colons (for emphasis)

   We found a solution: We would do the job ourselves.

C. Capitalize the first and last words of a title or heading as well as all other words *except*

1) articles (*a*, *an*, *the*)

2) coordinating conjunctions (*and, or, but, for, nor; so* and *yet* are flexible)

3) short prepositions (such as *in, on, of*)

   Advertising Strategy for the Small Business
   "Tax Shelters: Are They for You?"
   Introduction to Computer Programming
   "The Ups and Downs of the Adjustable Mortgage"

Note: Verbs such as *is* and *are*, although short, should be capitalized in a title or heading.

D. Capitalize the following:

1) names of specific persons, places, and things

   Reggie Jackson, like many famous athletes, also successfully maneuvered a career in advertising.
   A motor trip to Rome from Sicily would be an unforgettable vacation.
   The Eiffel Tower is the tallest structure in Paris.

2) names of organizations and institutions

   The convention of the American Psychological Association will be held during the week of May 3.
   Warren earned his bachelor's degree at Yale University.

3) historical periods, events, and documents

   Literature of the Renaissance is marked by an awareness of classical culture.
   The Revolutionary War began in 1775 and ended in 1883.
   The Declaration of Independence was adopted on July 4, 1776.

4) members of national, political, religious, racial, social, and athletic groups

The Republican candidate for mayor spent the morning shaking hands at the train station.
Babe Ruth was one of the most famous outfielders ever to play with the Yankees.

5) days of the week, months of the year, and names of holidays (but NOT seasons of the year)

I will have your order ready by Tuesday.
Wanda entered law school in September.
I always overeat on Thanksgiving.

(*but*)

Every summer, the Feins rent a cottage on Cape Cod.

6) compass directions used to refer to a region (but NOT used as directions)

Voters in the Northeast are often stereotyped as liberals.

(*but*)

Los Angeles is west of Las Vegas.

7) words referring to a deity or to religious documents

In Greek mythology, Zeus was the father of Castor and Pollux.
The Lord gives and the Lord takes away.
The Koran is the collection of Moslem scriptural writings.

E. Capitalize in these additional special situations:

1) regular nouns when they are part of a name

I worked at the corner of Twelfth Street and Arthur Avenue.

(*but*)

During lunch hour, the street was teeming with people.

2) adjectives that are formed from names

The American flag is a symbol of democracy.
Hamlet is a frequently produced Shakespearean play.

3) abbreviations of capitalized words

United Parcel Service—U.P.S.

(*but*)

cash on delivery—c.o.d.

4) titles that appear before, not after, names

The guests and Dean Douglas attended the first assembly of the year.

(*but*)

The guests and Paul Douglas, dean of students, attended the first assembly of the year.

    a) titles of *high* rank may be capitalized when used without a name

       The President of the United States held a press conference.

       (*but*)

       The president of American Motors held a press conference.

    b) terms of kinship may be capitalized when used as a name

       Before I went out, I told Dad that I'd be home by ten.

5) the pronoun *I*

    After the debate, I felt quite proud of myself.

6) the *first* word of a complimentary closing

    Sincerely yours,
    Yours truly,

Abbreviations

TITLES

A. *Mr.*, *Mrs.*, *Ms.*, and *Dr.* are always abbreviated when used before a name.

Mr. James Cooper	Mrs. Jane Bowles	Ms. Lillian Lewis
Mr. J. F. Cooper	Mrs. J. Bowles	Ms. L. Lewis
Mr. Cooper	Mrs. Bowles	Ms. Lewis

B. When the word *Saint* precedes the name of a Christian saint, it may be abbreviated; but when it is part of a personal name, the bearer's usage is followed.

St. Peter   St. Cecilia
Ruth St. Denis

(*but*)

Augustus Saint-Gaudens

C. Such abbreviations as *Prof.*, *Gov.*, *Col.*, *Sen.*, and *Rep.* may be used before a full name (a first name or initial plus a last name).

Prof. Fred Farkas *but* Professor Farkas
Gov. T. P. Barnes *but* Governor Barnes

D. The designations *Reverend* and *Honorable*, because they indicate dignity and respect, should not be abbreviated except in addresses and lists. Moreover, they must be used with a first name, initial, or title in addition to the last name.

Reverend Tom Payne	Honorable Bruce Ng
Rev. Tom Payne	Hon. Bruce Ng
Rev. T. Payne	Hon. B. Ng
Rev. Dr. Payne	

Using *the* before *Reverend* or *Honorable* indicates additional formality. When *the* is used, the designation is spelled out.

The Reverend Tom Payne   The Honorable Bruce Ng

E. Titles appearing after names must be spelled out, except *Esq.*, *Jr.*, *Sr.*, and academic, professional, and religious designations.

T. P. Barnes, Governor
T. P. Barnes, Esq.
Fred Farkas, Ph.D.
Tom Payne, D.D.
Wayne Redd, C.P.A.

COMPANY NAMES

A. Abbreviate firm names only when the company prefers it. Their letterhead will provide this information; for example, *Con Edison* is acceptable for the *Consolidated Edison Company*. Similarly, using & instead of *and* should be limited to the company's official use.

A & P   Lord & Taylor

B. The names of organizations and governmental agencies that are known by their initials may be abbreviated in writing.

The OPEC nations have agreed to raise the price of oil by another $2 per barrel.
The CIA has recalled its agents from the Far East.

TERMS USED WITH FIGURES AND DATES

A. The designation A.D. (*anno Domini*, meaning "year of our Lord") and B.C. ("before Christ") should always be abbreviated.

Claudius I was born in the year 10 B.C. and died in the year A.D. 54.

Note that A.D. precedes the year while B.C. follows it.

B. The abbreviations A.M. ("before noon") and P.M. ("after noon") may always be used.

My work day begins at 9:00 A.M. and ends at 4:30 P.M.

Note that A.M. and P.M. must always be used with figures. Do not use them with words or the term *o'clock*.

My work day begins at nine o'clock in the morning and ends at four thirty in the afternoon.

C. *Number* and *numbers* may be abbreviated as *no.* (or *No.*) and *nos.* (or *Nos.*), respectively, when used before figures.

The model I am most interested in is no. 131.
The following checks have not yet cleared: nos. 451, 454, and 458.

D. The dollar sign ($) is permissible in writing.

Ann owes Phil $19.95.

LATIN EXPRESSIONS

The following abbreviations are acceptable, though in formal writing the English version should be spelled out.

| cf. | compare | et al. | and others | i.e. | that is | vs. | versus |
| e.g. | for example | etc. | and so forth | viz | namely | | |

The major oil companies (Gulf, Exxon, et al.) are passing on the price increase to consumers.

OTHER ABBREVIATIONS

Certain words should not be abbreviated in letters, reports, or other writing. (In addresses, lists, tables, invoices, and the like, abbreviations are acceptable.) These words are:

1) Names of cities, states, and countries

   Although Arnold was born in Philadelphia, Pennsylvania, he has lived in Germany most of his life.

2) Months of the year, days of the week

   The shipment of electric yo-yos arrived Wednesday, October 1.

3) Parts of place-names, such as *Street*, *Avenue*, *Road*, *Park*, *Port*, *Fort*, *Mount*, *River*, as well as compass directions

   The Adirondack Mountains are northeast of the Mississippi River.
   The hardware store is on the west side of Bruckner Boulevard.

4) Units of measure, courses of study, and the words *page*, *chapter*, and *volume*

   On page 214 of the physics textbook, the speed of light is listed as 186,000 miles per second.

Numbers

A. Spell our numbers that can be expressed in one or two words; use figures for other numbers.

six million soldiers	6,490,000 soldiers
one-fourth	82¼
fifty dollars	$49.95

B. Certain numbers should always be spelled out.

1) Numbers that begin a sentence

   One hundred fifty yards of wire are needed to complete the project.
   We will need 150 yards of wire to complete the project.

2) Large round numbers

   six billion dollars

   or

   $6 billion

   (Using figures would imply emphasis: $6,000,000,000.)

3) Time expressed as a number alone or with the word *o'clock*

   four in the afternoon   four o'clock

   (Use figures with A.M. and P.M.: 4 A.M., 2:30 P.M.)

C. Other numbers should be indicated with figures.

1) Addresses: house, street, and ZIP-code numbers

   252 Ash Street, Greenville, Wyoming 71226
   11 East 49 Street *or* 11 East 49th Street
   P.O. Box 72
   RFD 2

2) Decimals

   6.293   0.00329

   (Note that commas are not used with decimals.)

3) Dates

   January 31, 1951

   or

   31 January 1951

4) Expressions requiring two numbers

   10 fifteen-cent stamps   2 five-dollar bills

   (Note that the first number is indicated in figures and the second is spelled out.)

D. Certain words and symbols are often used with numbers.

1) The word *percent* should be spelled out, except on invoices and lists (in which case you may use %).

   9 percent   11½ percent

2) The symbol ¢ should be used only in quoting prices. Otherwise, use words or units of a dollar.

   6¢   six cents $.06

3) The symbol # should be used only in tables, invoices, etc. Instead, use *number* or the abbreviation *no.* or *No.* The symbol should never be used with house numbers or RFD numbers.

Index

NOTES

NOTES

NOTES

NOTES

NOTES

NOTES

NOTES

NOTES

NOTES

NOTES

NOTES

NOTES